The Holistic Self™

*A proven program for healing
and realigning work-life balance*

JAMIE EAMES

ISBN: 1494241641
ISBN-13: 978-1494241643

DEDICATION

For Joshua, The Master Teacher

ACKNOWLEDGMENTS

To Michael for patiently working through the draft and providing valuable input and direction. Thank you.

Thank you Susie for your support and encouragement.

To Myles, thank you for showing me how to listen and trust the music in my heart.

To my Guides and Guardian Angels, our Friends from Ireland, thank you for your quiet companionship on the journey.

And we can't forget Matthew James, the Apprentices and The Three Fellas.

In memory and friendship of Beacon of Lorne, Shabala and Wurndjeri Children

To The Nothingness Where Everything Is, without you the journey and the book would not be possible.

i

TESTIMONY

"This is an enlightening and enjoyable read for anyone trying to navigate their work and personal life-path in a more fulfilled and authentic way. The approach and guidance provides many "Ah Ha" moments and prompts you to really challenge any self-defeating thinking or misguided beliefs about your value and potential."
Nik Halik – Author of *The Thrillionaire: Make Your Life and Epic Extraordinary Adventure*

" Jamie has done an amazing job with   ' The Holistic Self '. This book will draw you in and keep you turning the pages. I love the way it makes you feel empowered. It is a breath of fresh air. Women forget sometimes how to balance life and in this book you will find techniques that will change your life. Women all around the world need to read it."
Elise Quevedo – Author of *Creating a Kick-Ass Attitude*

"It was divine providence that I have met Jamie at the time of deep emotional and spiritual conflict and right after I stepped on the path of spiritual search. It was during our very first conversation when I was highly impressed with Jamie's sincere story of her own spiritual journey. I had no doubt in her calling to help people find their inner light, their true self. There is that wonderful and rare combination of inner light, wisdom, emotional and spiritual intelligence along with Jamie's knowledge and proficiency in modern technology that makes her stand out for me. She walked the walk and now offers me and other women an opportunity to learn from her experiences as she accompanies us on our journey. The Holistic Self will for sure change your life"
Alona Khorolska – North Carolina, USA

"For any woman looking to find balance in life, 'The Holistic Self' has a new approach that will not only uplift you, but transform the way you think. I now know myself in a deeper sense and it has helped me to find fulfillment and harmony in my work and personal relationships. "
Elena Rossi – Dublin, Ireland

CONTENTS

FOREWORD

The Holistic Self is an inspirational story of what happened to an ordinary person struggling to discover her authentic self and be true to her emotional and spiritual integrity. A phenomenon that occurred one night change the trajectory of her life-path, and was the impetus for what has now become a program that women – or men for that matter, can use as a framework to build a more empowering and harmonious life-path. It includes a series of easy-to-use templates based on years of study in the fields of spirituality, theology, astrology, and the behavioral sciences. These practical templates enable individuals to better manage their emotional and spiritual journey - which can often get subverted by today's often chaotic lifestyle. Experiential learning processes and tools build on methods the author devised to enable her to deal with her own struggles to be accepted as her true-self – a self she eventually came to love.

Spiritual Intelligence (SQ) is emerging as a key factor in the 21ˢᵗ Century, and you will read how the author's journey was influenced by insights and spiritual direction that brought harmony between her spirit, body, mind and heart. If you have ever felt disempowered or anxious, applying the skills and insights described in this book will promote a greater sense of control during situations that you may previously have found challenging, uncomfortable, or daunting. There is a specific section on EQ skill building which shows you how to quickly assess someone's personality type in order to build trust and credibility in work, social and personal situations. A major theme is the process of transformation between the first and second halves of life and how to map your life-path such that you are more self-assured and balanced without compromising your principals.

The Holistic Self is a resource that anyone who is on a quest to discover their authentic self will benefit from.

Raymond Arron – Author of
Double Your Income Doing What You Love™

COPYRIGHT

Liability Disclaimer

By reading this document, you assume all risks associated with using the advice given below, with a full understanding that you, solely, are responsible for anything that may occur as a result of putting this information into action in any way, and regardless of your interpretation of the advice.

You further agree that our company cannot be held responsible in any way for the success or failure of your business or personal matters as a result of the information presented below. It is your responsibility to conduct your own due diligence regarding the safe and successful operation of your personal and/or business relationships or associations if you intend to apply any of our information in any way to your business operations.

IF YOU DO NOT AGREE WITH THESE TERMS AND EXPRESS CONDITIONS AND THOSE ARTICULATED IN THE LATER 'DISCLOSURES AND DISCLAIMERS' SECTION, DO NOT READ THIS BOOK. YOUR USE OF THIS BOOK, PRODUCTS, SERVICES, AND ANY PARTICIPATION IN ACTIVITIES MENTIONED IN THIS BOOK, MEAN THAT YOU ARE AGREEING TO BE LEGALLY BOUND BY THESE TERMS.

1 SECRET PSYCHE COMPARTMENT

Have you ever been to a seminar or workshop where something the speaker says inspires a "THAT'S ME!" moment? I have, plenty of times and found myself making resolutions and plans for how I will definitely change my habits going forward. However, a few weeks or months later my motivation to get myself sorted out seems to fragment, or get overwritten by a new "Ah Ha!" moment as a result of seeing some quick fix on TV or hearing an inspirational speaker on YouTube.

Often when I encounter a moment of *awe* or even something that causes me to make a split decision to change a long held perception, I wonder to myself, how did I end up here? Only when I slow down and reflect on that question do I gradually begin to see a pattern emerge. However, it requires real effort and focus to take the threads of that pattern – which may have been uncovered during a moment of reflection, or glimpsed in my peripheral vision as I walked through a forest – and weave them into my day-to-day conscious awareness. It's even more difficult to try living my newly upgraded life pattern authentically and not get dragged back into self-defeating old habits.

What do I mean by 'living it'?

I notice that day-to-day living demands my complete dedication and effort to survive, and any *awe effect* I encounter is more often than not soon pushed aside. Those rare moments of awe quickly get buried beneath the spectacle of television, video games, or movies that bombard our senses. I know, for example, that computer-generated images are shallow and false, and yet I have allowed myself to lazily accept them as substitutes for the authentic miracles that are more subtle and less intrusive. I feel that I am progressively less capable of registering moments of awe because those rare things of deep beauty and immeasurable value are lost in the glare of shallow and crude imitations.

Sadly, even the word 'awesome' has been hijacked and dumped into a marketing meat-grinder along with most other superlatives that were sparingly used a hundred years ago. However, I have discovered that those rare and priceless moments of awe perpetually reside in their quiet and gentle state deep within our *Secret Psyche Compartment* (SPC). Those moments are buried so deep that they are not formally registered in my intellect as having ever existed, but they are accessible in other ways.

What happens when I bury something in a compartment?

It fills up!

When my SPC is full, it nudges against the wall of consciousness and demands some liberation. That is, it demands my conscious attention.

How can I give something I've completely forgotten or misplaced any attention?

"Very good question!" She says to herself.

Fortunately for my sanity and wellbeing *Life* does not forget. She remembers. She is the keeper of all the exceptional moments that reside in the SPC. She hears their pleas and acts for their release at the appointed time - like a lawyer in a court who advocates for the release of someone who was mistakenly incarcerated. However, *Life* doesn't judge or adjudicate but simply facilitates completely out of Love and Compassion. She has no personal investment in gain or loss. She has no reputation to protect. She has no secrets to hide or ego to satisfy. She acts purely in a state of Love and Compassion.

How does *Life* take action after hearing a plea to be released from the SPC?

"Another good question!" She happily exclaims.

She facilitates appropriate circumstances to enable me to remember those lessons I learned during the moment of awe (even if fleetingly).

"This is the complicated part!" Who said that? (Maybe that was *Life* whispering?)

If *Life* just sends an ordinary day-to-day circumstance to get my attention, she would be drowned out - just like the gentle voices in the SPC, and I would fail to hear her. She needs to up her volume, sort of speak out a bit. She needs to yell loud enough for me to hear her above the rattling voices of other people's everyday demands, excitement or distress that intrude on my liminal space. That secret and sacred space, or threshold, between my past and future states where I seek the meditative calm – the **now** that is so elusive in today's hyperactive world.

What kind of circumstance is powerful enough to jolt me out of my life-path routine?

"Joy and Sorrow" comes the reply... (I think that was *Life* whispering loudly.)

I experience joy in moments of personal awe and I experience sorrow in moments of personal suffering. Different people have different perspectives of joy and sorrow. Hence, it must be 'personal' to be an authentic awe experience.

This is a story of how *Life* reminds me to listen to the voices in my SPC and subtly suggests how I might apply her prompting in my daily living. *Life* acts only out of Love and Compassion, she gives me plenty of training before she fully opens the lid of my SPC. *Life* has to compete (tolerate is probably more accurate) with my ego's assertion that I've got all I need, and so patiently waits for me to be ready to deal with whatever gift *Life* is about to facilitate.

This is not a theological essay, nor is it intended to convince or convert you to any particular faith, religion, or empirical fact. The first half of the book is a story of one person's journey in the company of her companion – *Life*. The second part (Chapter 5 onwards) outlines the tools, methods and insights I uncovered that helped me on my *journey into self discovery* and I hope they will be of value to you the Reader.

If you believe you are at the beginning of your own amazing journey and sense the presence of your very special companion - *Life* (or another name that your heart recognizes), and you find that my journey is starting to resonate with you, you will know that you are not alone. It's of course entirely your choice to follow along on this account of my *journey into self-discovery*, or step off and return to your comfortable ways. If you choose to continue reading, we can share a fellowship of gifted living that I choose to call *The Holistic Self.*

2 WHO AM I?

Who am I?

Such a simple question contains limitless answers – it just depends on where you want to start, how much you want to disclose (or are afraid to share), and the context of the environment that motivated the question.

More often than not when we are asked who we are, we respond with what we do: "I'm an entrepreneur," "I wrote a best seller book," "I'm an actress who is between gigs and likes to improve her acting method in a diner – it's where the real people are found." Alternatively, we answer who we are relative to someone else: "I'm Theresa's sister," "I'm Joshua's mother," or "I'm Dean's wife." We seldom have a personal 'elevator pitch' that answers a question about our core identity, and even if we did, it would likely be a greatly diluted version of that core identity.

As part of my introduction, I think it's important to disclose up-front my intent relative to how I view the relationship between myself as the author and you as the reader of this book. I believe you are the only one who is qualified to decide if the book content has relevance or value. Many people may feel that the experiences I share in the following pages are not credible, are contrary to a particular religious belief, or are simply too esoteric. Some may even dismiss them as the ramblings of a misguided mind because it doesn't align with their world-view. I always assume such comments are well intend, but if not, then I can't control that – nor should I try.

Be assured that I have questioned my sanity and motivation many times during and especially after a mystical experience I was blessed to be a part of. I have presented myself with the full range of reasons and rationale why I shouldn't publish my experiences many times. However, after years of deliberation the only reason I felt justified sharing my story and insights was to provide support for people who struggled with an 'unexplainable' event or felt disconnected in some way. Therefore, my intent is to offer a safe haven where people can take shelter as they travel their own often turbulent and unforgiving life-path. Maybe I can provide some direction or a frame of reference that makes the journey forward a bit easier. In any event, all I'm offering is a glimpse into one person's private journey that hopefully will help my readers to find some 'Ah Ha'" moments or a way to get on with life with less stress.

> "Do not believe in anything simply because you have heard it.
> Do not believe in traditions because they have been handed down for many generations.
> Do not believe in anything because it is spoken and rumored by many.
> Do not believe in anything simply because it is found written in your religious books.
> Do not believe in anything merely on the authority of your teachers or elders.
> But after observation and analysis, when you find that anything agrees with reason, and is conducive to the good and benefit of one and all, then accept it and live to it."
> — The Buddha

I finally feel comfortable disclosing some of the factual details about myself – something I would have avoided like a plague even two years ago. However, I suspect you will need some general insight into the *nature, nurture, culture and free-choices* that influenced the direction of my life-path before you invest your emotional energy in this text. The good news is that you don't have to disclose anything yet – that comes later (if you're still engaged with the text) when you'll have an opportunity to face yourself in a true mirror and be asked to disclose your authentic-self to yourself.

I was born in Thailand of native Chinese parents and the eldest of four children. Traditional Chinese culture does not place a high value on a daughter and although my parents loved and cared for me as best they could, that culture imposed many limitations on what I could be expected to do. Of my early childhood I recall occasional moments of fun and happiness but it mostly centered on blaming myself for being female. However, I finally decided that I could aspire to being more than a disempowered girl. My rebellion started early; the carefree happy child became a crusader.

Mine was a community occupied by honor along with 'buying status' and 'saving face.' The expectation was that girls would not finish college but assume a housewife role. These expectations and how older relatives attempted to influence my parent's decisions, made it difficult to go to university and complete a degree in Biochemistry.

> "The ultimate liberation is to be liberated from the identification with being a woman. My womanhood is not the deepest thing that can be said about me. The deepest thing is that I'm a living trajectory of divine purpose and compassion moving through this time and space dimension in this form, and one of the names that I bear is woman. But it is not the whole of the consciousness."
>
> - Cynthai Bourgeaulty, The Meaning of Mary Magdalene

After completing my undergrad study, I engineered my way into an airline hostess job that lasted a year. This was principally to finance my ambition to pursue further study in the United States. The airline experience served me well as a relatively secure environment to build my competencies in English and awareness of Western culture. So when I arrived at the University of Texas in Dallas, I was not overly intimidated by the change in environment or by having to work in a local country club to pay my tuition and living expenses. I completed my post-graduate study in Information Technology and returned to Thailand to work.

I eventually married an American man who worked at the same technology company I did in Thailand and we had two children. My daughter was born prior to moving back to the United States, and three years later my son was born. One standout challenge I recall is shoveling the morning snow in our driveway during winter in Massachusetts before going to work, but I like to think it helped to build the character and resilience my future life-path would demand.

To other Thai-Chinese women, I had a Western lifestyle that would have been the envy of many, but there was a core part of me withering away beneath the materialistic overlay. Who people really are 'behind closed doors' no one truly knows and we are not well equipped to self-diagnose the many causes of a fragmenting union. In retrospect, if I knew about *Social Style* or the *Enneagram* back then, it might have been easier to avoid a lot of the relationship tension that started to build – or at least put non-judgmental labels on our incompatibility. In any event, we went back to live in Thailand in 1994 but eventually divorced. Both my ex-husband and I committed to place the interests of our two children ahead of our differences, and while there was mutual civility and respect the consequences of that divorce had a widespread impact on all of us.

Until 1998, my brothers and sister owned a prominent IT business in Thailand and I joined as a general manager after working with a number of multinationals. Success was building quickly and our company was regularly featured in the local newspapers and business magazines as a market leader and authority. This success resulted in my father 'walking tall' among our neighbors and relatives and seemingly regained the 'lost face' of a pre Chinese Revolution nobleman. However, just as everything seemed prosperous, my life-path suffered another major blow.

> "You have traveled too fast over false ground;
> Now your soul has come to take you back
> Gradually, you will return to yourself,
> Having learned a new respect for your heart
> And the joy that dwells far within slow time."
> — John O'Donohue, *To Bless the Space Between Us: A Book of Blessings*

I had just about recovered from the emotional and financial train-wreck that resulted from walking away from my seemingly 'perfect' marriage, when less than two years later my family's business folded. In 1997 the devaluation of the Thai Baht to less than half of its US$ equivalent caused an economic crisis. The crisis spread throughout Southeast Asia and it was later jokingly dubbed the *"Tom Yum Khung Disease"* after the famous spicy Thai soup. One year later, my family's IT systems business collapsed and my brother and sister filed for bankruptcy. I was already out of a job at that stage and not until later did I realize that this circumstance was the start of a more enlightened life-path for me. Sadly many businesses and some lives were lost as a result of that financial crisis – mainly due to people's inability to cope with the loss of material artifacts, life savings and social standing.

In the midst of struggling to recover from what seemed like a personal and business implosion, I tried to make sense of why it all happened. Back then it looked like it could be anything from some type of punishment, a universal message, or even a bizarre midlife crisis.

> "There is the solitude of suffering, when you go through darkness that is lonely, intense, and terrible. Words become powerless to express your pain; what others hear from your words is so distant and different from what you are actually suffering."
> — John O'Donohue, *Anam Cara: A Book of Celtic Wisdom*

As my father's home had been used as collateral for the now bankrupt business, the bank initiated the process to repossess it. As my sister and brothers were financially insolvent, it fell on me to take a job to support my family. This ultimately required me to move to Singapore. I left without my children to minimize the impact on them. Words could not describe the crisis my family and I went through but the financial implication was so huge that we were forced to sell everything we owned. Sacrifices had to be made to just survive, at the same time that we tried to 'save face' by keeping the true impact of our family's material demise from our neighbors' prying eyes. In hindsight, many of those neighbors were oblivious to our situation as I'm sure they had their own challenges to deal with.

For the next year I spent too much time trying to analyze the circumstances that led me to receive a double-blow to my 'karma'. I stopped all social activities. The self-imposed exile in Singapore ironically eased my humiliation somewhat as no one knew my personal circumstances there. I chose isolation rather than friendship, which ultimately proved self-defeating as I felt increasingly alone and outcast. Gradually I sensed a well of anger begin to take root deep inside of me. It seemed to be waiting for its chance to erupt if I showed any weakness. So I called on all my stubbornness and proven resilience to contain the rumbling aggression that was seeking release.

My spare time became filled with searching for answers to the unexplained suffering in my life. I read and studied any relevant publications and enrolled in programs that claimed to illuminate the mystery of Life. This included Tarot, Palmistry, Astrology, Energy and Crystal healing, Philosophy, Psychology, Sociology, Quantum Physics, World Religions, and so on. I was lost and could no longer identify my true-self or reclaim my past certainty of who I was. Trying to hide from the awkward quality of my seemingly downward financial spiral became almost an obsession. In the depth of my self-pity, I was unaware that for years I had been travelling over false ground and that my soul had to come to take me back.

> "One of the most beautiful gifts in the world is the gift of encouragement. When someone encourages you, that person helps you over a threshold you might otherwise never have crossed on your own."
> — John O'Donohue, *Eternal Echoes: Celtic Reflections on Our Yearning to Belong*

I first met my current husband at work while living in Singapore. He surprised me by pointing out my positive attributes and encouraged me to continue being me. Like a few drops of rain falling onto parched earth, my spirit instinctively shook off its crust and rose to receive his encouragement. That was to be the turning point of the other path to discover my authentic self - but I hadn't yet realized that I had also found my soul mate who would soon be sharing my life-path's new trajectory.

"Two roads diverged in a yellow wood,
And sorry I could not travel both
And be one traveler, long I stood
And looked down one as far as I could
To where it bent in the undergrowth;

Then took the other, as just as fair,
And having perhaps the better claim
Because it was grassy and wanted wear,
Though as for that the passing there
Had worn them really about the same,

And both that morning equally lay
In leaves no step had trodden black.
Oh, I kept the first for another day!
Yet knowing how way leads on to way
I doubted if I should ever come back.

I shall be telling this with a sigh
Somewhere ages and ages hence:
Two roads diverged in a wood, and I,
I took the one less traveled by,
And that has made all the difference."
— Robert Frost, *The Road not Taken*

3 HOW DID I GET HERE?

During the usual breakfast chat with my (second) husband one morning recently, I suddenly realized we were behind schedule to get one of his books finished. As we jumped up from the table we simultaneously asked, "How did we get here?"

> "All the possibilities of your human destiny are asleep in your soul. You are here to realize and honor these possibilities. When love comes into your life, unrecognized dimensions of your destiny awaken and blossom and grow. Possibility is the secret heart of time."— John O'Donohue, *Anam Cara: A Book of Celtic Wisdom*

Mulling over my past, I systematically ticked off some success criteria. I am a proven business analyst and project manager in the corporate technology field and have worked on many highly demanding and complex projects. I also have a strong multi-cultural background from living and working in a variety of countries and building close friendships with many diverse people across the globe. Of course it wasn't all plain sailing and I was met by failure on more occasions than

I'd have liked – but mostly I managed to learn from those mistakes (sometimes it took a few times for the message to sink in). I called it "my school of hard knocks". However, I believe I've generally managed to reengage with life in a more positive and holistic way largely due to the inner calling of my heart. This is probably the time when I started to actively pursue spiritual intelligence awareness – which eventually resulted in my formal studies of the SQ21 method a year ago.

It took time but I gradually learned to become aware of when I was behaving in an ego-centric manner and also to recognize that such behavior was the consequence of fear-based thinking that the Enneagram later helped me to manage. Fortunately, through study, meditation, guidance and my school of hard knocks, I uncovered a way to *press pause* on my self-defeating behavior. In those brief moments of pause, I would insert love-based signposts to help me adjust my direction onto a more healthy and balanced path. This re-orientation of my normal re-active habits into pro-active methods was not an overnight accomplishment – far from it. My *journey into self-discovery* - that I now call *JiSD*™, only really commenced when I discovered the key to getting my finger on that 'emotional pause button' (in the fraction of a second before I would previously have reacted). The instruction I received on how to achieve this *better way* was from a source that many would find difficult to believe.

Yet, I can't help asking myself again as I arrive at this point in writing my book: Now what? At times during my earlier drafts I'd question my sanity. What on earth am I doing? Am I insane to ask the reader to believe that I could actually hear "a voice"? For the hundredth time I ask - am I the victim of some mysterious neurological illness that caused a certain part of my brain to be more active than usual, like John Travolta's character in the movie *Phenomenon*?

My questioning usually takes a tour of my husband's view, my financial and security concerns, and eventually lands in the middle of the reality of our limited funds. I often feel we're crazy to spend all our spare money, and often scraping the bottom of the credit card barrel, on studying various disciplines, buying a mini-library of books and courses, moving from country to country with only a few months' notice. However, beneath all of this self analysis, my *heart* knew something profound was happening so I felt compelled to keep going on this journey.

The conversations around more than a dozen different kitchen tables over the past ten years were often bathed in tears and firm resolutions that if our reward didn't appear by the next deadline, then all bets were off with this faith stuff!

Eventually, we just got tired of protesting and 'woe is us' pageants and strangely just evolved into accepting that "there's no thinking required, let's just get on with it!" To some extent my casual interest in *scientific astrology* (which I also later pursued in depth during a two year program with a master practitioner) helped me to accept hard to justify phenomena. Most people simply accepting that the moon affects the sea currents and the seasons influence the behavior of the animal kingdom, so just extending this thinking allowed me to accept that cosmos energies permeate all living things – and that my nature was partially preset. What I gradually learned was that all I have to offer is faith and trust. I have faith that my soul knows what she is doing. I know intuitively that the 'voice' is not me and I'm not the voice and yet we are one. It is what the mystics called the paradox. I know and yet I don't know – and it's ok.

The destiny that is asleep in my soul has been awakened and I am fulfilling it and yet I don't need to know what that destiny is. I uncovered my truth in the words of Clarissa Pinkola Estés

> "It is worse to stay where one does not belong at all than to wander about lost for a while and looking for the psychic and soulful kinship one requires"
>
> — Clarissa Pinkola Estés , *Women Who Run With the Wolves*

My restlessness to follow the *road less travelled* was not a conscious thing for a long time. Initially I thought I was being pushed away from places where I felt misunderstood because I daren't risk being called a 'loony' if I shared my inner voice, but later I understood I was slowly and gently being drawn towards *the psychic and soulful kinship one requires*.

One evening when I was living in Singapore, I got up at 2am for no reason. I call it my '2-3am' wake up call. I have noticed that the 'Unconscious' communication with my conscious self is most pronounced between 2-3am. I was working on my personal computer that morning when I heard a rattling sound at my patio door as if the wind was shaking it. I thought a storm was on its way and continued with my work. The rattling noise started again and this time it sounded a bit unusual so I got up to look outside. It was a clear night, no rain, no wind, and no sign of a storm. When I got back to my desk, I heard a voice inside of me like I was listening to a conversation with myself, except I was not. The voice said, *"Go to knock."* If you feel like putting the book down because the story is getting a bit peculiar, I wouldn't blame you. I thought so too at the beginning and shook my head to dislodge what I felt must be a symptom of sleep deprivation.

As I worked away with all my faculties operating like it was 3PM not 3AM, the inner voice kept repeating, *"Go to knock"*. I tried to work even more intensely, getting ahead of my following day's work, but the voice quietly persisted and it was starting to drive me crazy. I finally took a risk and asked *It* quietly, *"Where* do you want me to go to knock?" Sadly there was no response to my question. Out of curiosity one day, I *googled*, "knock" and aimed my focus on a 'place' since that would make sense in the context of 'go to.' To my surprise, there was a place called "Knock" in Ireland, in the northwest area. It was near the border between Counties Sligo and Mayo.

It seemed the *voice* was asking me to go to Knock in Ireland. I didn't know where it was or how to get there. I'd

never been to Ireland and would not know where to start –
not that I was intending to go there. However, I was wrong
and restlessness started to build inside over the next month as
I felt the urgency of the calling escalate.

> "As we enter the path of transformation, the
> most valuable thing we have working in our
> favor is our yearning."
> — Cynthia Bourgeault, *The Wisdom Jesus : Transforming Heart
> and Mind--A New Perspective on Christ and His Message*

I asked around to see if someone at work knew anything
about Ireland and Knock in particular. One of my work
colleague mentioned that Enda, whom I'd been working with
for a few months, was Irish. I thought he was Australian as
he lived in Melbourne and commuted to Singapore as he held
a regional responsibility for Asia. I was faced with the
dilemma of how much to reveal to Enda about my strange
phenomenon of hearing a voice that couldn't be
substantiated. How do you tell someone you hardly know
that 'a voice' is telling you to go to a place called Knock? I
avoided the matter as I didn't want to face the possibility that
he would think I was at best a bit strange and at worst
someone that he should report to the personnel department
for help…Yikes!

I had no choice really. The urgency that nagged at the core
of my being sort of encouraged me to just ask for his help. It
sounded easy in theory but the inner *fear-voice* warned me that
it wasn't straightforward and would likely end in disaster as I
hardly knew him. I eventually resolved to do it (as there was a
real scarcity of Irish people in Singapore from what I could
see) but needed to build up my courage to reveal my
'strangeness.' After a lot of rehearsals in front of my mirror,
and a few more non-starts due to a herd of butterflies
fluttering manically in my stomach, I was as ready as I would
ever be. The next time Enda was in Singapore, I decided to

tell him the truth, as much of it as I was willing to share with him anyway.

To my surprise, Enda never flinched when I blurted out my question and said he knew Knock very well as it was near his hometown. He enthusiastically spoke about Knock's main attraction, which was the Marian Shrine where Mary the mother of Jesus is reported to have appeared to over a dozen local people near the end of the 19th century. Enda seemed genuinely interested in my story and for someone who was generally talkative (some would say too talkative), he said very little while I was talking. In the end he said he believed me and surprised me, again, by saying he'd accompany me to Knock. I didn't know it then but Enda was to become a great friend, and eventually my husband.

> "You do not need to know precisely what is happening, or exactly where it is all going. What you need is to recognize the possibilities and challenges offered by the present moment, and to embrace them with courage, faith and hope." — Thomas Merton

Thomas Merton was right. I took a risk to *embrace* my mysterious request *with courage, faith and hope,* and the Universe sent me a helper.

Weeks before I left for Ireland, I attempted to engage in 'conversations' with the *voice* (some people would call it a prayer) but didn't place much hope on receiving any reply. Yet another surprise, I received a clear instruction during another 2:30am wakeup call. The *voice* said, "Go to the old chapel and kneel down. Someone who knows you will meet you." If you think the last message was unbelievable, this one topped the score. What did it mean if I went through the trouble of getting to this place and knelt down and no one showed up? What would that say about me? Scary thought... There was also the small matter that Knock is a revered Christian holy place and I was a devout Buddhist!

Leading up to the departure for Knock, I had a recurring dream of heavy rain on a gravel ground. It became etched into my memory and I could recall it on demand with crystal clarity. When I arrived at Knock on December 31, 2001 it was raining. The parking lot of the Knock Shrine was exactly like what I had seen in my dream – "rain on a gravel ground."

There was a chapel called the Old Chapel against which the glass-fronted Apparition Shrine was built. I went into the old chapel and walked around in anticipation of making eye-contact with someone who was also seeking some unknown. No one approached me and no one looked my way. I was ready to accept defeat and declare myself insane, when I recalled a part of the message that I had not yet fulfilled, to kneel. I went to the front of the chapel, knelt down and bowed my head in prayer. As I looked up to leave, I saw right in front of me the carving on the altar of Our Lady Mary as she was holding Jesus's body. My eyes were drawn to a face and I started shaking and was overwhelmed by joy. "Someone who knows you will meet you." Quietly, with tears streaming down my face I confessed, "It's You I've been looking for. I'm home."

> "It could be a meeting on the street, or a party or a lecture, or just a simple, banal introduction, then suddenly there is a flash of recognition and the embers of kinship glow. There is an awakening between you, a sense of ancient knowing."
> — John O'Donohue, *Anam Cara: A Book of Celtic Wisdom*

I returned to Singapore and my transformation began to accelerate. There were many more messages and unplanned trips – most of which were in Enda's company as he had become enveloped in his own spiritual reawakening.

I moved to Ireland shortly after. I was at a crossroads in my career in 2002 as my company was fragmenting and most of my valued workmates were made redundant – including

Enda, so I eventually resigned. I kept in touch with Enda and when he found an opportunity to work in Ireland that needed my type of skill and experience, I agreed to go there for a short time. The opportunity to spend time in a place of spiritual significance for me and to work on an interesting project had great appeal. I have lived in the United States, Hong Kong, Thailand, and Singapore, so I felt moving to Ireland would not present a major challenge.

Soon after arriving in Ireland, I met a Jesuit priest who was willing to be my spiritual director. He provided me with a rich insight into authentic Christian practice and he encouraged me to harmonize it with my Eastern faith. This led to my deep engagement with Anam Cara – a spiritual companion method that takes the non-judgmental approach that I speak about later in the book. He was the person who introduced me to the Enneagram personality type method as a way to build empathy with others as well as to a *therapeutic* Neuro Linguistic Programming (NLP) program. This was invaluable during his patient and non-judging way of guiding me onto the path of discovering who I truly am. He reassured me that to be holistic means to be free and recommended that I take a year to study full-time in Theology and Spirituality at the Milltown Institute. He said to me, "You have beautiful music inside that needs to be shared. You can only do so when you learn the language to communicate the music with others."

I spent the next ten years learning the language to share the beautiful music inside me – so that others are encouraged to find the language that speaks to their hearts. *The Holistic Self*™ program is partly a hymnbook where people can share their inner music and connect their own inner voice to others. It was in Ireland that I entered my transformation phase or what I now call the *Ulysses Paradox*.

4 WHY AM I AFRAID TO TELL YOU WHO I AM?

"If I expose my nakedness as a person to you
– Do not make me feel shame."
— John Powell, *Why Am I Afraid To Tell You Who I am*

Since I was young, I have had a sense that no one truly 'sees' me. It's frustrating when I can't seem to get my point across. I used to joke with friends and work colleagues that I needed a universal translator, like the one in the Star Trek movies, to help me communicate my intent and insights in business and personal situations. Therefore, for the past ten years I have been in search of my universal translator - not something sophisticated like the one Mr. Spock uses, just one that would allow me to share my mystical experiences in a faith-neutral language.

After completing a one-year program in Theology and Spirituality at the Milltown Institute in Dublin, I followed on by attending a 2-year program in Ignatius Spiritual Direction at the Jesuit's Manresa center. By this stage my life had changed dramatically. My original reasons for coming to Ireland were overtaken by a profound motivation to really delve into Celtic Spirituality and my traditional Buddhist faith seemed to sit comfortably alongside my new Christian beliefs.

I felt compelled out of gratitude for the awakening I received to offer my companionship to others who were seeking the type of guidance I received from my spiritual director. This all occurred alongside various work opportunities that I secured that eventually took me into the Cloud Computing space.

Living in Ireland for nearly six years and being close to Knock, and many other sacred places throughout the country, was a blessing. My 'cup' was filled to the brim. Ireland, *"the land of saints and scholars,"* had given me the deep heartfelt knowledge that enabled me to transform into *who I already am.* The best way I can explain it is that I was able to get my ego-self under better control by discovering and embracing my higher-self. It was a gradual process like how waves crash upon the seashore and gradually creep up the beach to seep gently into the sand and rest. I started with understanding Social Style and the Enneagram as a way to build self-awareness and managing my compulsive ego-centered reactiveness. Then I progressed into uncovering the key insights into integrating that self-awareness with my journey into self-discovery. It eventually led me to seeing a number of patterns that would form the basis of what I share later in this book, and which helped me achieve greater harmony in my work, social and personal life.

During this period, I met many *'seekers'* on similar quests to myself. We crossed paths and made ourselves known to each other in different ways. Some I encountered during a class discussion, at a spiritual retreat, or simply in a chance encounter that evolved into a conversation about a topic of mutual interest. They all helped me to feel I belonged in their community. I was one of them. I was home.

> "I will arise and go now, and go to Innisfree,
> And a small cabin build there, of clay and wattles made:
> Nine bean-rows will I have there, a hive for the honey-bee;
> And live alone in the bee-loud glade.

And I shall have some peace there, for peace
comes dropping slow,
Dropping from the veils of the morning to
where the cricket sings;
There midnight's all a glimmer, and noon a
purple glow,
And evening full of the linnet's wings.

I will arise and go now, for always night and
day
I hear lake water lapping with low sounds by
the shore;
While I stand on the roadway, or on the
pavements grey,
I hear it in the deep heart's core."
— WB Yeats, *The Lake Isle of Innisfree*

Just as I was feeling settled and connected to the Irish way
of life, another message came knocking – quietly at first but
soon more persistent. It was more a 'proposal' than a request
that asked us to move to Australia. We did not want to move
again and had settled into what we thought was to be our
final destination. We even placed a deposit on a cottage
beside our favorite lake after spending a short period in
southern England. Even though we know that *the voice* is the
voice of love and compassion, the reason for our various
tasks is never disclosed. We had come to the stage where we
no longer think about the *why* or *how* and so we eventually
found ourselves transitioning into a preparing to depart
process. We knew the path wouldn't be easy but formally
confirmed our *heart's* choice to accept the 'proposal' by
booking flights and house movers. The next step was to start
looking for work opportunities that would allow us to migrate
to Australia.

We usually uncover the real reason for the proposed move
in hindsight, a few years on when we start seeing how the

moves fit into a bigger tapestry that includes, for example, why we moved to England for nine months. In hindsight, I now see why I secured a new type of role with that Cloud Computing company less than a year before we left for Australia. It was against all the odds and in a most unlikely series of scenarios that resulted in a major strategic career move.

Prior to getting the job, I wanted to stay in my comfort zone and retain my authority and credibility in old-school ICT roles, but there were limited opportunities after returning from England. I therefore had to swallow my pride and re-engineer myself in the full glare of my young hot-shot colleagues. Once I got the hang of what was involved I discovered that the reason I was hired was in fact due to my business analysis and customer empathy and not for technical wizardry – the company had that in droves.

It seemed like I experienced recurring *déjà vu* moments that built upon on another year after year. I was again getting glimpses of a bigger spiritual tapestry within which my tiny contribution was somehow worth highlighting. So when the time was approaching to make our move *down under* it felt like all the obstacles we encountered coming to Ireland were facing us again on the path to Australia. Enda again assumed the role of our appointed scout to find the quickest and safest path for us. If it could be done, I knew he'd find a way.

The road to migration proved to us once more that our wise ancestors know the secret to holistic living. We gain nothing from an easy journey. Like our physical muscles, emotional and spiritual muscles also need exercise and a challenge to build their strength. The mystics call the spiritual exercise path, the *'path of descent.'* In Richards Rohr's *Seven Themes of an Alternative Orthodoxy*, Theme 6 states; "The path of descent is the path of transformation. Darkness, failure, relapse, death, and woundedness are our primary teachers, rather than ideas or doctrines."

Melbourne, Australia is a lovely place to live and after another chaotic move (we seem to always encounter every possible obstacle in this sector of our life-path) – and with Enda's enduring optimism and my stubborn resilience – we settled into a comfortable routine. After resigning from the company I worked with in Ireland, I managed to get hired by the company's Asia Pacific group who were based in Sydney. Fortunately, circumstances resulted in the need to open a Melbourne branch office so I only spent a month in Sydney while Enda set up his scout camp in a cheap apartment in Melbourne. As usual we were scraping the bottom of the barrel of our finances but Enda said he wasn't fazed because he needed to finish the thesis for a post-graduate degree he started eighteen months previously in England.

The extra time he had for uninterrupted study enabled him to intensify his research and achieve a breakthrough in the area of behavior and personality type. A core element of our future work together is a direct result of that thesis work - which is now called *Your Visible Personality*, and something we practice on a daily basis to maintain awareness of how our different 'world views' can potentially cause tension and misunderstandings.

During the first year with my new company, I wanted to be accepted into the team environment and was afraid to 'rock the boat'. I also had a similar goal for home life and did whatever people in my local community did. I wanted to blend in and be like most Australians so I tried to be neighborly and participate in outdoor activities. I also went to church and volunteered for good causes. In other words, I projected the 'normal' side of me. However, I didn't have access to my Irish spirituality group anymore and although my new friends were kindhearted, welcoming and supportive, I felt I couldn't really reveal my type of 'spiritual language'. I gradually found I was retreating back to how I would hide my true self before I went to Ireland, and back to doubting my spiritual experiences.

My belief in the voice started to diminish as I was afraid that other people would laugh if they knew I could hear a 'voice'. I found myself being elusive when people asked why we moved to Melbourne because I couldn't openly admit that we blindly followed the *voice*. Kabir Edmund Helminski in *Living Presence: A Sufi Way to Mindfulness & the Essential Self* said, "Today there is a resistance to religious and traditional language by a great number of intelligent people. This is not necessarily a resistance to the truths religious language formerly expressed, but to the cheapening and conventionalizing of Reality." I did not believe that a single person could change the tidal wave of *the cheapening and conventionalizing of Reality*. I was afraid of being ridiculed if I started to share the truth about my experience.

I knew my work background and resume of experience would enable me to be accepted and safely blend into the shallow veneer of an Internet technology environment. I told myself that having a Cloud Computing job and being able to speak the trendy 'language' of social media would allow me to be perceived as authentic. Although I helped various people to resolve a myriad of issues during my journey through many countries these past twenty years, it was mostly 'underground' work. Those in need didn't ask for my CV, they just needed a hand, any hand, to reach down and help them climb out of a particular hole. I was good at listening and helping people with emotional and spiritual challenges but I felt like a fake, like I was usurping someone else's role. I believed I had a gift but was afraid to tell people who I really was in case they thought of me as a freak, or a charlatan, or that I was delusional.

Even though I got away with telling Enda about the *voice* on that fateful day in Singapore, I convinced myself that I couldn't expect to be that lucky twice. So I kept the *voice* to myself and Enda but constantly worried that I would be caught out someday and ridiculed. John Powell in his book mentioned that, "If there is no one who understands me, and who accepts me for what I am, I will feel estranged. My talents and possessions will not comfort me at all. Even in the midst of many people, I will always carry within me a feeling of isolation and aloneness. I will experience a kind of solitary confinement."

In my reluctance to reveal my integrated self, and even though the people I helped were very grateful (many of whom were refugees from 'accredited' or 'certified' institutes), I allowed my SPC to be filled to the limit.

> "It is better to live your own destiny imperfectly than to live an imitation of somebody else's life with perfection."
>   – *The Bhagavad Gita*

As I mentioned earlier, *Life* who is compassionate and loving, intervenes on behalf of my inner self, amplifying the inner voice that is muffled by society's clamor or the often blaring protests of my ego-self. I started to catch small whispers at first but when I listened more closely and with a quieter mind during my return to a meditation routine, the sound of a familiar voice started to penetrate my materialistic dome. The restlessness to be respected and acknowledged for who I truly am started to return and I felt more and more like a misfit in my environment. I started to become unhappy when materially I was in probably my most healthy state for decades. The gradual downward spiral of my emotional health started to manifest itself physically. I progressively got sick and acquired a variety of disabilities that the doctors could not conclusively diagnose as the result of a particular illness.

The problems persisted and expanded to the extent that some doctors suggested that perhaps it was 'all in my head' and recommended I take time off from work to reduce my stress levels. However, my body was unrelenting at sending signals to me that something else was wrong. Perhaps my original biochemistry studies had made me overly loyal to staying with the scientific method for diagnosing a problem, so I continued to ignore any bodily warning signs. Eventually, *Life* facilitated some circumstances to stop me from continuing my downward spiral towards serious disablement by engineering a breakout for the residents of my SPC.

I had two highly complex operations within a six months period – one to fix my vertebrae and another to replace my hip. The stress of investing so much effort and money trying to uncover a cure for my physical self triggered an emotional switch that caused me to get caught up in a vicious whirlwind of fear. The sicker I was the more our financial pressures mounted. This led to the thinking that the option of prematurely going back to work would make me feel better. I had convinced myself that topping-up our bank account would solve my emotional anxiety as my stress levels had now overshadowed my physical pain, but I was wrong. Unconsciously, I was screaming "Why can't I tell you who I am?" at the world, and this became a conscious realization while I was lying on my back in the hospital. Something had to change.

Mary Oliver eloquently describes the irony of a human being's wish to be someone other than ourselves.

> "I would be a fox, or a tree
> Full of waving branches.
> I wouldn't mind being a rose in a field full of roses.
> Fear has not yet occurred to them, nor ambition.
> Reason they have not yet thought of.
> Neither do they ask how long they must be roses,
> and then what.
> Or any other foolish question."
> — Mary Oliver – *Roses, Late Summer*

I laughed at such a notion because I now know that is precisely what I was doing. I was afraid to tell people who I am because I was ashamed of being me!

Is it my fear of revealing my authentic-self, or my ambition to live my egotistic-self that has caused me to be incapable of moving on? Fear...?

> "If you try to view yourself through the lenses that others offer you, all you will see are distortions; your own light and beauty will become blurred, awkward, and ugly. Your sense of inner beauty has to remain a very private thing."
> — John O'Donohue, *Anam Cara: A Book of Celtic Wisdom*

I found courage to change the lens of my worldview and changed the '*distorted mirror*' I extracted my reflection from. I left my work in the technology sector and reinvented myself. I leveraged my knowledge and experience in Cloud Computing into a much tighter area of focus in social media and online business support. However, that was principally to enable me to get my message out to the world, to honor my core gift and proudly tell anyone who is interested who I am. My public profile now reflects this gift and the once second-tier Asian female, who was trained to know her place, has transformed into a confident and empowered global citizen who embraces her *holistic self*.

I found comfort in the words from Herman Hesse's, *Siddhartha*: "The world is not imperfect or slowly evolving along a path to perfection. No, it is perfect at every moment, every sin already carries grace in it" Everything is perfect the way it is, my imperfection is made perfect in grace. I choose to reveal my true self without shame or guilt.

I reengaged with studies in spirituality and theology again and was accepted into the first cohort of Richard Rohr's *The Living School* which entails the studying of non-dualistic, contemplative spirituality. I studied Emotional Intelligence (EQ) and Spiritual Intelligence (SQ), obtaining certification as an SQ21 coach, so I can now legitimately help others develop their Spiritual Intelligence skills. I've founded a faith neutral program called *The Holistic Self*™ *Program*, which has the intention to accompany and inspire others who are seeking a way to embrace and reveal their own holistic selves.

> "The world is, therefore, more real in proportion as the people in it are able to be more fully and more humanly alive: that is to say, better able to make a lucid and conscious use of their freedom. Basically, this freedom must consist first of all in the capacity to choose their own lives, to find themselves on the deepest possible level."
> – Thomas Merton, *Love and Living*

5 THE ULYSSES PARADOX

I spent many years in search of a *language* that would enable me to 'bare my soul'. Since the day I left Thailand, I progressively improved my command of English to the extent that it is now my de facto tongue. However, the regular incidents of miscommunication relating to how people perceived my intent, or misalignment of eastern and western cultural nuances, drained me emotionally. It often seemed that I was operating on a different wavelength to other people and that the usual combination of words, tone of voice and body language wasn't enough to enable a reasonable channel of communication.

It was like digging a railway tunnel through a mountain from either side. If I didn't get the communication and alignment right I would end up with two tunnels and a lot of blame and finger-pointing. However, I started to feel that my issue wasn't about two tunnels but three, so even if I did a good job aligning and empathizing with another person's perspective, I still felt that I had an extra pathway unconnected. It's like an electric plug with a positive, negative and earth pin, but the socket in the wall only has two slots – it can work but it just doesn't line up cleanly or effectively a lot of the time.

Richard Rohr constantly reminds his students that if *we are not transformed by our painful experiences we almost always transmit them.* John O'Donohue had a similar concept about transformation and he said it a bit differently. He saw transformation as *a human soul longing to be seen.* I often thought how I might enable something I'm not fully aware of, or can describe properly, to be seen – but I actually get where he's coming from.

> "By definition, soul evades the cage of definition... It can never be touched and yet the merest hint of its absence causes immediate distress."
> — David Whyte, *The Heart Aroused*

Eknath Easwaran wrote in his introduction to the Upanishads that like strangers in an unfamiliar country walking every day over a buried treasure, day-by-day we enter that Self while in deep sleep but never know it, carried away by what is false. My soul is a stranger in my waking moment and how I allow my soul to be seen is to 'bare my soul'. This is similar to the way I pay attention to the memories trapped in my SPC – those moments of awe or deep suffering that I glimpsed or experienced.

> "If you hate a person, you hate something in him that is part of yourself. What isn't part of ourselves doesn't disturb us."
> — Hermann Hesse, *Demian*

A good metaphor for the relationship between my soul and my persona is the Ulysses butterfly. When a Ulysses butterfly spreads its wings, the beautiful bright blue against black colours of the wings' design attracts our attention. Most of the time we don't see the subtler brown and grey colours on the underside of the wings until it is in its non-flight mode, or at rest. My soul is like the subtle side of the Ulysses butterfly. Building on the same analogy, the butterfly cannot always be flying. It needs time to regain its energy by resting on a twig or a branch and in doing so folds its wings to blend into the background. My soul and my persona have a similar relationship – two sides of the same 'holistic self'.

The first half of my life was like the beautiful brightly coloured side of the butterfly. My objective was to be seen; to be recognized; to be admired and to attract attention, in other words the path of ascension or *traveling fast on false ground*. The second half of life, I tended to be more subtle, considered, and less demonstrative as *my soul had come to take me back*.

How did I know that I was going in a wrong direction?

First, I needed to pause and get a general idea of where I was in the current moment, and try to recognize familiar landmarks so that I could orient myself. I probably had been moving along without conscious thought and letting the momentum carry me – until I had a strong sense that I was lost. If I were driving, I'd have found a place to stop and either consult a map or better still use the GPS (Global Positioning System) or Sat-Nav on my mobile phone or one installed in the car. After turning-on the GPS system I'd enter my destination to "get pointed in the right direction".

The first thing the system does then is ask me where I wish to start from (as it doesn't yet know my current location). I choose the option that says "this location" and then the process of determining where I am starts. The GPS device has a chip that contains data (current location, device type, etc.) and 'sprays' that data-packet up to space where it is intercepted by at least four communication satellites. These satellites compare the data they each receive, talk to each other, filter out non-relevant data to isolate the 'common' points of reference, and then calculate where the GPS device that initiated the signal is located. After those four satellites agree, they send a signal back down to the GPS saying "*Hey! You're currently in this location Jamie!*" I then click the "start guidance" option and my GPS 'voice' instructs me on the optimal path to follow to get me back on track to my desired destination.

Many times I have felt isolated and lost in situations that have caused me to become disoriented and frightened. I found I had somehow wandered off the right path or been misdirected into 'dark' places. I wished then that I had a map or a *Life-Path GPS* to illuminate my path so that I could quickly get myself realigned with the direction I should have been heading. When things started to fall apart during the second half of my life journey, it was *Life's* signpost, which alerted me that I was getting lost, moving away from my soul's destination.

Despite continuing to move in what I perceived to be the 'right' way, as it had served me well enough during the first half of my life, things suddenly began to fall apart. I got divorced, my family's business collapsed, and I got separated from my children while they were still very young. I had to leave my family, my friends, and all that I called 'home' due to circumstances that I felt were not entirely of my own making. The human logic and rational thinking that helped me to navigate my life-path to that point was no longer working. All my familiar landmarks and signposts seemed to get misplaced or concealed in shadows and I could not make sense of my life anymore.

The Ulysses Butterfly's metamorphosis from caterpillar through the pupa stage into the butterfly is probably the closest metaphor for my own life-path. The butterfly egg contains the pre-programmed information for all three stages of its lifecycle. This data is stored in a small nucleus is the blueprint for building and operating a caterpillar; for the pupa transformation stage, and for the development and operation of the butterfly. In the pupa cocoon, the caterpillar uses up its reserves of energy and slowly transforms into a new body design and life purpose. The metamorphosis cannot be rushed and the process takes as long as the pupa requires.

When the right time arrives, the former caterpillar struggles with all its strength and instincts to break-free of the cocoon to emerge in the shape of a butterfly. It is this life and death struggle to be free of the cocoon that enables the former caterpillar to build the required strength in its wings to support its new persona in flight.

On the one hand, the caterpillar dies when it enters its pupa cocoon so that it can be re-born into the new form and the second half's life mission of the butterfly. On the other hand, the caterpillar does not fully lose its core identity, just its shape, persona, and mission. The struggle inside the cocoon to get free and become a butterfly only happens after the caterpillar voluntarily relinquishes its former physical attributes and habits for a higher purpose. In nature, if a caterpillar does not go through the transformation process it ceases to exist. It physically dies and many caterpillars never reach their butterfly potential.

I was like a little caterpillar that used to happily eat her way through a leaf in the same garden and at the same time of day, until one day the once satisfying food no longer gave her joy and she found herself entering the *pupa* stage. I entered mine in 1995. Unlike the fatalistic caterpillar, my human transformation process had the gift of being offered a free choice at each stage to:

1. Ignore *Life's* signals and signposts and remain where I was
2. Deny there are signals and signposts and struggle to go back to where I was
3. Acknowledge the signals and signposts to trustingly surrender into the transformation process.

I called my transformation process *The Ulysses Paradox*. It is a paradox because:

- Both the first half and the second half of life are true;
- They need each other to exist;
- The outcome does not invalidate either half of life; rather it integrates all aspects and experiences into what it was ultimately born to be. In other words an authentic person integrates all life experiences in a free choice manner to eventually become their holistic self – to various degrees.
- The Ulysses Butterfly had all it needed to exist when it started out life in its caterpillar persona – intrinsically it was *both/and* not *either/or*

A caterpillar is born to be a butterfly. A human person is manifested physically, spiritually. My holistic self is inclusive of my physical, mental, emotional and spiritual attributes; my bright colourful persona, my shadow and my soul.

"We stumble and fall constantly even when we are most enlightened. But when we are in true spiritual darkness, we do not even know that we have fallen." – Thomas Merton

Major religions have different names for the *'die to self'* transformative process. Buddhism calls it *Samsara* – the cycle of birth-death-rebirth. Christianity calls it the Pascal Mystery of Jesus's death and resurrection. The common denominator is free-choice and how we exercise that in harmony with our nature and nurture will largely determine how we travel our life-path.

The *Life-Path GPS* is a set of insights and tools to help people to more easily navigate their life-path. They are offered as an interconnected and harmonized suite of resources that when practiced daily help you to orient yourself in moments of confusion or conflict relative to your work, social, personal or spiritual path. It equips you with skills you can use to navigate and illuminate your path especially during the dark nights. I use these tools myself to discern and understand where I should journey and who I am as a *holistic person*.

In a similar manner to how a car or phone GPS works, a *Life-Path GPS* also needs points of reference to help set the trajectory of the onward journey. By continually checking your alignment with critical milestones on the route you have selected, you reduce the incidents of getting disoriented or lost, and increase the likelihood of reaching your targeted destination (or state) sooner.

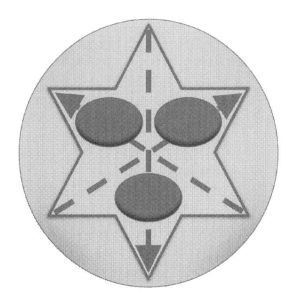

Unlike the GPS which needs at least four satellites to determine a physical location, *The Holistic Self* approach uses what I call *An Integrated Double Triangulation*© method or *AIDT*©. This concept is represented by the 'The Holistic Self Symbol' that references the three key 'STAGES' someone needs to gain knowledge of if they are to increase the likelihood of achieving their *holistic-self's* potential.

The three stages are:

- *Your Visible Personality*™ *(YVP*™*)* – to understand your personal parameters;
- *Journey into Self Discovery*™ *(JiSD*™*)* – to plot the optimum life-path relative to your personal parameters;
- *Anam Cara* or *Spiritual Companionship*

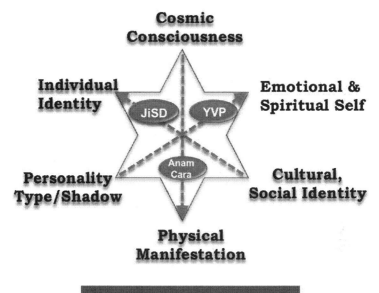

Cosmic Consciousness

Individual Identity

Emotional & Spiritual Self

JiSD YVP

Anam Cara

Personality Type/Shadow

Cultural, Social Identity

Physical Manifestation

The Holistic Self

There is a fourth factor that I use to complement the other three reference points. It is how *Universal* forces and energy influenced my life-path trajectory at the start of my journey. It provides me with a way to identify my original anchor reference against which the other three are calculated. However, there is one critical piece of data required to make it either very useful or simply just another curiosity. That piece of data is my time of birth. It's analogous to the *version* code on a 'chip' inside the car's GPS unit.

The critical *time stamp* is coordinated with my date and location of birth, and without it I have significantly lower accuracy when it comes to determining my original life-path potential and trajectory (i.e. my *nature*) – prior to my *nurture* and *free-choice* factors being introduced into the equation. This factor is Scientific Astrology and even if you don't have your exact birth time, there are resources that I have access to that can assist in finding a *likely* time.

At this stage in the book, you may feel the urge to EXIT and grab the local newspaper, check out the daily astrology section, grab some data that you are told will '*plot your future path in the stars*' and with this revelation in hand you set off with unbridled optimism. To be honest, I did start off that way to a certain extent and jumped onto the Internet (that's what we did back then but the content was not as rich as it is today), read some books, enrolled in classes and waited for the fruits of my efforts to unfold.

Unfortunately that short-cut approach didn't work out as I had hoped, so I eventually felt compelled to retrace my steps and do the work properly. I refined my research and tried out various combinations of resources, while simultaneously trying to survive and maintain my sanity. Fortunately, *Life* facilitated circumstances whereby I became receptive to my soul *calling me back*. The less superficial approach I took proved to be very rewarding as ten years later I arrived at *The Holistic Self*.

If you're happy to spend weeks and months trying to patch all the above referenced information together that is of course your free choice, and I genuinely hope you only have slight adjustments to make to achieve a very fulfilling life-path. However, most people I have mentored and coached on *The Holistic Self* method tell me that their *solo-efforts* (before our sessions) at finding a better life-path caused them to be frustrated, stressed, confused, agitated and angry… and that's only in the first month!

When I started out on my journey, all I wanted was a simple, fast and easy system to help me start:

- Having the courage to make decisions;
- Not living in constant fear and guilt;
- Having deeper and more meaningful relationships;
- Feeling more empowered and recognized for my true worth

I believe I have distilled decades of information – and smashed my fair share of plates, keyboards and pencils (the new plastic ones) in the process – to compile a template and method that actually works right now for misfits and other misunderstood members of the human species. People like me!

> "No one else has access to the world you carry around within yourself; you are its custodian and entrance. No one else can see the world the way you see it. No one else can feel your life the way you feel it. Thus it is impossible to ever compare two people because each stands on such different ground. When you compare yourself to others, you are inviting envy into your consciousness; it can be a dangerous and destructive guest."
> — John O'Donohue, *Anam Cara: A Book of Celtic Wisdom*

6 EMOTIONAL & SPIRITUAL INTELLIGENCE

Emotional Intelligence (EQ) is primarily about operating from an empathetic position and is underpinned by a willingness to step out of your own shoes and into those of someone you are different from emotionally. We use EQ to ease tension and misalignment during a negotiation, a social event, or in a personal relationship. Empathy comes more easily to some people than to others – but it is a learnable skill. Improving your EQ helps you gain a better understanding of what motivates you and other people to behave the way you do, and how your approach might have either a positive or negative impact on others.

Most people don't know their own personality type, so being able to determine it, and also that of others, is a highly valuable skill at work, socially, and especially in close personal relationships. The need for a stronger focus on improving our EQ in the workplace is highlighted by the increase in sick days attributed to stress that are clocked up by workers across all business sectors today.

"We live in digital time. Our pace is rushed, rapid fire and relentless. Facing crushing workloads, we try to cram as much as possible into every day. We're wired up, but we're melting down."
— Jim Loehr, *The Power of Full Engagement*

EQ competency is no longer limited to face-to-face communication or the domain of the *personnel department*. In today's business or personal environment, building EQ competency is a strategic initiative that must embrace all channels of communication. Even China is highlighting the importance of EQ as a competitive advantage in the global marketplace. When the question "Intelligence quotient and emotional quotient - which is more important?" was put to Chinese President Xi Jinping, he said, "EQ is important for adapting to society, although it should be used together with professional knowledge and techniques."

It's no wonder therefore that there is an accelerated effort by businesses to engage in EQ coaching as a way to achieve a competitive advantage. There is also a greater emphasis in management training programs to restore the 'human face' to business leadership. David Whyte, in his book *The Heart Aroused – Poetry and the Preservation of the Soul in Corporate America* highlights the compelling need for a deeper discernment on the nature of work.

"It seems that all the overripe hierarchies of the world, from corporations to national states, are in trouble and are calling, however reluctantly, on their people for more creativity, commitment, and innovation. If these corporate bodies can demand those creative qualities which by long tradition belong so directly to our being, to our soul, they must naturally make room for their disturbing presence within their buildings and their boarders." — David Whyte, *The Heart Aroused*

This talk of soul and spirit might sound somewhat idealistic to the more 'bottom line' or pragmatic individual, but perhaps the idea of a place for spirituality is only recognized in a work context when we are on the receiving end of some less than ethical or personally compromising situation. The adage *"Know thyself"* in a work context is about achieving an understanding of *why* behaving out of your 'comfort zone' can either have a positive or negative effect on colleagues or clients. The old approach of 'one-size-fits-all' is no longer tolerated in a product or solution offering – because customers have a vast array of choices, so why would it be acceptable in a relationship management situation?

Just because I'm highly focused on making sure that all the items on my 'to do' list are ticked off by the end of a workday doesn't mean that everyone else should have the same priority. Such a 'task' centred focus could result in high outputs in the short term, but it could also cause a dramatic reduction in productivity (and profit) because the stress levels in the enterprise become unacceptable as a result of an overzealous manager. Sometimes pressing 'pause' on my 'to-do' list so that a team-member can receive an emotional lift can deliver greater profitability.

Being able to discern when to back-off on the task list in favour of emotionally resuscitating a colleague very often results in a spike in overall productivity. Such empathy and compassion can earn 'brownie points' in the form of the recovered colleague going the extra mile outside normal work hours to help the team achieve an unrealistic deadline. This example is called applied EQ but it's not as simple as group hugs ever second day, it's about tuning into what Daniel Goleman calls "resonance".

> "Resonant leaders know when to be collaborative and when to be visionary, when to listen and when to command. Such leaders

have a knack for attuning to their own sense of what matters and articulating a mission that resonates with the values of those they lead. These leaders naturally nurture relationships, surface simmering issues, and create the human synergies of a group in harmony."
— Daniel Goleman, *Emotional Intelligence*

Your Visible Personality™ is about applied EQ and is the result of a research project conducted by Enda Eames that distilled and summarized volumes of information, strategies and approaches in sociology, psychology and related areas. The objective was to produce a practical and easy to use method that helps people build trust and achieve more harmonious and productive relationships, and it delivers on this if all the feedback from my clients is to be believed. The central theme is centered on helping *laypeople* to build and apply Emotional Intelligence skills in a relatively quick way so that they achieve better relationships in their work, social, or personal life.

The *Your Visible Personality* concept was developed on the premise that there is a correlation between what we can observe in a person's behavior and what has been researched about the different motivations that people have, which are ultimately reflected in their personality. The term *Your Visible Personality* is a substitute for a string of descriptions of how behavior, personality, the conscious, the unconscious, core identity, and the hidden attributes of the human construct interact and integrate.

The approach centers on using *Social Style* to interpret someone's behavior (their body language, tone of voice and the pace or energy of their words) then translating this information into one of nine *Enneagram* personality types.

Knowing someone's likely personality type (without them disclosing or even knowing it themselves) allows you to approach them in such a way that it keeps tension low, comfort and/or productivity high and increases the possibility of achieving a "win-win" outcome.

Social Style has two dimensions – "assertiveness" and "responsiveness" (the word "emotiveness" is substituted by some practitioners). Assertiveness is defined as: "*the degree to which a person is perceived as attempting to influence the thoughts and actions of others.*" It can also be explained as "the degree to which a person appears to ask questions or make statements (tell) in interactions with others." Responsiveness is defined as: "*the degree to which a person is perceived as expressing feelings when relating to others.*" It can also be explained as 'the degree to which a person reacts reflexively to influence or stimulation – displaying (emoting) or concealing (controlling) emotions during an interpersonal encounter'.

The study of Social Style assists you to better understand and apply knowledge relative to your own and other people's visible behavior by building competence in a model of four styles - the "*Driver*", "*Expressive*", "*Amiable*", and "*Analytical*".

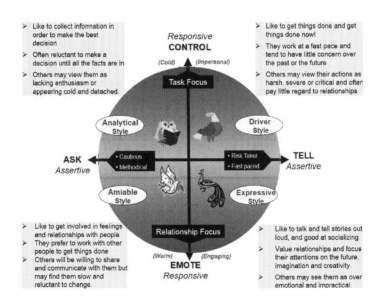

A key Social Style concept is modifying your own behavior in order to "reduce interpersonal relationship tension" (Wilson Learning) that can occur when people of different social styles are negotiating or interacting. Therefore, to become better aligned with the expectations of other people, we need to have a means of estimating their 'internal motivations,' and a strategy for adapting our approach in response.

At a practical level, an Expressive, when dealing with an Analytical (their opposite style), should slow down their pace of speech; be more focused on task details (rather than the 'big picture'); be patient and listen without too much interruption; and show respect for their research and conclusions – generally be less animated and entertaining. The key point is to understand how the other person prefers to engage, so that you (as an Expressive) can adapt your own style to be more compatible with how the Analytical likes to operate. If you can identify the other person's style – by just observing their behavior, you are less likely to annoy them, or create tension, when you start interacting. It's about having a plan for a pro-active engagement – and sticking to it.

The Enneagram relates to a graph of nine personality profiles, or *types*, that represent a distinct, well-developed coping strategy for relating to self, others and the environment. It has been described as *"a map of the lower emotional center – or the domain of passions"* (Naranjo). Each of the nine types also has its own precise path to psychological and spiritual freedom.

The Enneagram is not a new phenomenon in the area of psychology and has been described as a reawakening and reformatting of insights about personality that have existed for over two thousand years. As a framework for understanding how people interact, it is very relevant in today's society, whether in a business, social or even a spiritual context. It assists people to have greater empathy for different perspectives and to make sense of why people behave differently. It also helps us self-diagnose our 'blind spots' – the self-defeating behaviour that cause us to *get in our own way*, and which often results in a lot of interpersonal tension or stress. The nine Enneagram types are divided into three sub-groups that correspond to the three Centers of Intelligence (Head, Heart, and Body), through which information is processed.

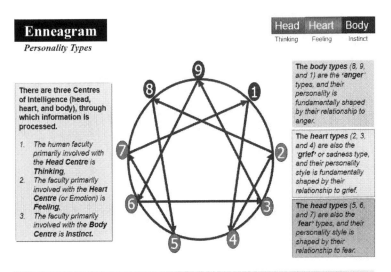

The types on the inner triangle (3, 6, and 9) are also called the core points. Thus, type 3 is the core of the Heart Centre types; type 6 is the core of the Head Centre types; and type 9 is the core of the Body Centre types

The Enneagram symbol dates as far back as the works of Pythagoras. It was incorporated by both the Christian *Desert Fathers* relative to their analysis of the "capital sins"; and the Islamic *Sufi* schools which taught "the awakening to diversity within humanity ...a process of self-effacement in which the false-self, the ego, vanishes" (Jironet) around the 4th Century.

The Enneagram lay dormant for a long period until it re-emerged in the *West* through the Jesuits. It was largely kept secret for centuries but was subsequently reintroduced into public awareness by such teachers as G. I. Gurdjieff, the originator of a school of spiritual work near Paris in the

1930s, and Oscar Ichazo, a Bolivian philosopher. It is the latter who is credited with developing the Enneagram symbol that we know today and his "Protoanalysis" teaching - a comprehensive analysis of *the complete human being*, identified how a person's ego becomes established into patters during our childhood. This work was ultimately represented as the nine personality types on the Enneagram diagram. Claudio Naranjo, a Chilean-born, American-trained psychiatrist, studied Ichazo's teaching and further developed it in the seminal publication *"The Enneagram of Society: Healing the Soul to heal the World"*.

Naranjo then brought his understanding of the Enneagram system to Berkeley University, California in the early 1970s, where he taught it to students such as Helen Palmer who said: *"The Enneagram enhances, affirms and augments other psychologies and training methods.... is self-verifiable, lending itself to scientific psychology. Determining our personality type through the Enneagram does not put us in a box, but instead helps us see the box from which we view the world, so that we can step outside of our limited perspective and constraints. By gaining a better sense of how we have unknowingly and automatically constrained ourselves, we can develop healthier relationships, lead more productive and fulfilling lives, and experience our true essence."*

An understanding of personality type is a valuable resource when trying to decipher the differences between people – especially what motivates their unexpected behavior. A central theme of the Enneagram is that everyone has intrinsic value, and is blessed with strengths and virtues that must always be treated with understanding and respect.

The reality that people are more likely to behave in certain ways if their interests are being satisfied, is similar to how our behaviors reflect the motivations that are associated with our personality type. These motivations in turn are reflective of the defensive or fear based strategies that we acquired as a child to protect ourselves in a number of situations. Richard Rohr, OFM in his lecture series *"The Enneagram, The*

Discernment of Spirits", contends that our 'personality type' is probably made up of "one third nature, one third nurture, and one third free choice".

The *nature* attributes could be described as our 'universal programming' or what some people refer to as energy patterns, astrology, spirit, and even our DNA encoding. However, we also bring our well established cultural and heritage bias or *nurture* to all interpersonal encounters, and it takes a conscious effort of will to minimize their influence or even to be conscious of their impact – especially during stressful or confrontational situations. Therefore, the most flexible and adaptable element of our make-up is *free choice*, and this is the primary conduit through which negotiation between two people can most healthily take place.

The nine Enneagram types are divided into three sub-groups that correspond to the three *Centers of Intelligence* (Head, Heart, and Body), through which information is processed.

- "The human faculty" (or gift) primarily involved with the Head Center is thinking; the faculty primarily involved with the Emotional (or Heart) Center is feeling; and the faculty primarily involved with the Body Center is instinct.
- The three Centers of Intelligence also correspond to three core emotions that influence the character of the types.
- The Head types (5, 6, and 7) are also the *'fear'* types, and their personality style is shaped by their relationship to fear.
- The Heart types (2, 3, and 4) are also the *'grief'* or sadness type, and their personality style is fundamentally shaped by their relationship to grief.
- The Body types (8, 9, and 1) are the *'anger'* types, and their personality is fundamentally shaped by their relationship to anger.
- The types on the inner triangle (3, 6, and 9) are also

called the core points of each center's triad of types. Thus, type 3 is the core of the Heart Center types; type 6 is the core of the Head Center types; and type 9 is the core of the Body Center types."

Everyone needs to improve their EQ skills and for many the Enneagram provides the best track to run on. It is increasingly used by business leaders, psychologists, counselors, government diplomats and others during negotiations and presentations. It is even used by actors and movie stars to help them to achieve greater empathy with the personality of the different characters they play. This is very evident when you see how leading actors become so immersed in their character that they can come across as authentic and highly credible in a variety of different roles.

The following is the core concept that underpins the *Your Visible Personality* method:

PURPOSE:
- *Social Style* helps us to **understand** how people like to be interacted with – based on their **observable behaviour** (i.e. how they behave).
- The *Enneagram* helps us to **understand** the emotions and feelings - **the personality types,** that underpin and influence our Social Style behaviour. It explains what is important to one personality versus another.
- Through an understanding of how Social Style and the Enneagram integrate, we can increase the **efficiency and effectiveness** of our **interpersonal relationships** with others and achieve 'win-win' outcomes in 'negotiations', personal relationships, socially and at work

PROCESS:
- We first **observe a person's behaviour** in order to identify their Social Style (Assertiveness & Responsiveness). This will help us determine if they are an Analytical; Driver; Amiable; or Expressive.
- Having narrowed our options, we **match** what we know about the selected **Social Style** to the descriptions of the different **Enneagram** types.
- By **reducing the Enneagram types to 2 or 3 possibilities,** we increase our ability to empathize with another's perspective (i.e. putting yourself 'in their shoes'), so we can understanding how our type's personality impacts them
- We adapt our own approach to build trust, reduce tension and get aligned

PAYOFF:
- People will view the same situation (i.e. a problem, conflict, opportunity, proposition, negotiation, etc.) **through one of 9 different 'personality lenses'.** Knowing what motivates people at a 'personality' level helps us to approach a situation from their perspective, and address their priorities.
- Adapting to other people's 'world view' **increase our ability to influence** and more effectively **achieve a 'win-win'** (or *win-perceived win*) outcome

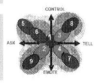

The first stage in the process is to identify an individual's Social Style, followed by determining which Enneagram types are aligned with that Social Style. It is not possible to guarantee a perfect match, so the objective is to narrow down the possible Enneagram types you are dealing with through a process of elimination. For example, if you can determine that the person you are observing is an *Expressive*, then it is likely you are dealing with an Enneagram type 7 or 4.

There are a number of key points to keep in mind when you are 'profiling' someone – such as making allowances for the 'healthy' and 'unhealthy' state of the person you are observing. While this might sound difficult to do, it is relatively straightforward when you have a template or cheat-sheet to work with. A very useful resource that contains easy to understand and use templates and infographics that explain the symbiotic relationship between Social Style and the Enneagram types is *Personalities at Work*™ Kindle eBook.

Skill at narrowing down the likely types will increase by continually observing the degrees of *assertiveness* and *responsiveness* during interactions with people and through building familiarity with type descriptions. However, figuring out someone's type is only half the story, the other part is to get them to collaborate. It is worth remembering that people will only step out of their 'comfort zone' (i.e. their usual behaviour pattern or habits) if there is a good chance they will get a return on their effort to be flexible or collaborative. People need to be able to envision some type of reward for such flexibility, and in business it is often an intangible personal benefit such as *recognition* (expressive); *approval* from peers (amiable); *respect* as an expert or an authority (analytical) or *control* of a situation (driver). Generally, offering tangible benefits such as a wage or salary increase, a promotion, or even to remain employed doesn't seem to work as effectively as an emotional reward for many relationship oriented people.

People who are successful in leadership, socially or in their personal lives have typically demonstrated empathy and understanding for those they interact with. They have usually taken the *punishment* of putting their own agenda on the 'backburner' in order to allow the other person to 'win' first, thereby gaining a *reward*. In business, this reward can be winning a sale, getting a project delivered, negotiating a contract, etc. Socially and in personal relationships it can be greater harmony or a deeper bond. Those who don't practice empathy and flexibility usually find it more difficult to build relationships because effective teamwork and collaboration requires empathy and versatility as a critical success factor.

Staying in our comfort zone (i.e. applying the same old inflexible methods) or taking the risk to move out of it (i.e. being flexible and adaptable) is a matter of personal choice. Ultimately, you will only change your approach if you have a personal motivation to do so. Therefore, if you need to get something achieved through another person's effort, or are seeking to build a more trusting relationship, the onus in on you – as the recipient of the benefit, to identify what will motivate the other person to buy into your proposed approach. Knowing another person's Social Style, and in turn their Enneagram type, will significantly improve your ability to communicate the type of specific benefits that are likely to motivate them to go along with your proposal.

It's important to note that you can't take a manipulative approach using the *Your Visible Personality* method because people will instinctively figure out when they are being manipulated. Integrity is so important when interacting with others because their sub-conscious is working away in the background observing how your body language, tone of voice are aligned or in conflict with the words you are using.

Therefore, an empathy mindset (with integrity) in conjunction with the *Your Visible Personality* method will help you to anticipate with a high degree of accuracy WHAT approach is likely to be most appealing to someone whose behavior you are seeking to influence (ethically). It also helps you understand WHY their priorities or focus is different or similar to yours; and HOW to best approach them in a way that quickly reduces tension, builds trust and creates a comfortable and productive social or working environment.

The Enneagram as a resource to increase your EQ knowledge and awareness, is proven to deliver excellent results. For this reason, the *Personalities at Work*™ Kindle eBook is used as a key reference during the *The Holistic Self*™ *Life-Path Mentoring Program*. I use it to help clients to quickly become proficient in Social Style and the Enneagram because of its easy to follow approaches and templates. It's like having the combinations of a GPS in your car along with clearly marked signposts and road markings to help you navigate unfamiliar winding roads - something especially valuable during times of poor visibility or bad weather conditions. In a similar way, without reliable signposts and guidance your relationship management journeys can be much more challenging, precarious and stressful – especially when you need to quickly build understanding, trust or collaboration.

The material in the Your Visible Personality book (that the *Personalities at Work* eBook is a subset of) is unique in terms of validating how sociology (behaviour) and psychology (personality) are inter-related and symbiotic. The method references such outstanding texts as:

- *"The Enneagram: Understanding Yourself and Others in Your Life"* by Helen Palmer. Perhaps the best in-depth exploration of the theory and application of the types.
- *"The ABC of the Enneagram"* by Eric Salmon. Adapted from his French text and explains the Enneagram types through light-hearted cartoons (see templates below).
- *"Bringing out the best in yourself at work"* by Ginger Lapid-Bogda. This book is the definitive business centric text on the Enneagram, and articulates how personality attributes are aligned with *forming; storming; norming* and *performing* roles in team building.
- *"Personality Types"* by Riso & Hudson, which also offers a free *online personality profiling tool*.
- *"Social Styles"* and *"Managing Interpersonal Relationships"* by Wilson Learning.

Another pivotal element in the *The Holistic Self*™ programs is a Spiritual Intelligence or SQ resource called *SQ21*. This assessment tool provides the means to measuring someone's capability across 21 Spiritual Intelligence skills that have been validated by many respected authorities. SQ awareness (or "Advanced EQ" as it is sometimes referred to), is now considered as important for leaders as high IQ and EQ skills, strong business acumen and good delegation skills. Leaders need to be able to *discern* the best ways to maintain a high performance culture and have staff intrinsically motivated to consistently give their best effort. Therefore, SQ cross-referenced and aligned with *Social Style* and the *Enneagram* provides a much deeper and rounded perspective of both team and leadership performance. The assessment output also provides insights into the overall health of an enterprise.

"The focus is not on types of people, but types in people."
— Don Beck (and Christopher Cowan), on Spiral Dynamics.

SQ21 is the result of a major 12-year research effort that is based on "*Advanced EQ and Spiral Dynamics*" theories and practices. The Author, Cindy Wigglesworth draws a lot of her influence and insights from what she refers to as "the great mystics and sages", from Rumi to Jesus, from Krishnamurti to the Dalai Lama, as well as Jung, Maslow, Ken Wilbur, Daniel Goleman and others. Her definition of spiritual intelligence is:

"The ability to behave with wisdom and compassion, while maintaining inner and outer peace, regardless of the situation... I believe we are all born spiritual, but we are not born spiritually intelligent. Spiritual Intelligence takes work and practice. In the same way, a child may be born with musical talent, but unless she learns the skill of playing an instrument, and practices her art consistently, she will not grow up to be a great musician." —Cindy Wigglesworth

SQ is not specific to any particular religious practice and is therefore 'faith neutral' (or none). Many religious leaders are now taking the view that the *content* is more important than the *container* when it comes to applying spirituality within a religious context.

In 2010 an article in the New York Times, titled *"Many Faiths, One Truth"* Tenzin Gyatso, the 14th Dalai Lama said:

> "When I was a boy in Tibet, I felt that my own Buddhist religion must be the best — and that other faiths were somehow inferior. Now I see how naïve I was, and how dangerous the extremes of religious intolerance can be today... An early eye-opener for me was my meeting with the Trappist monk Thomas Merton in India shortly before his untimely death in 1968. Merton told me he could be perfectly faithful to Christianity, yet learn in depth from other religions like Buddhism. The same is true for me as an ardent Buddhist learning from the world's other great religions. A main point in my discussion with Merton was how central compassion was to the message of both Christianity and Buddhism. In my readings of the New Testament, I find myself inspired by Jesus' acts of compassion... Take Judaism, for instance... I remember vividly the rabbi in the Netherlands who told me about the Holocaust with such intensity that we were both in tears... In my many encounters with Hindu scholars in India, I've come to see the

centrality of selfless compassion in Hinduism too — as expressed, for instance, in the Bhagavad Gita, which praises those who "delight in the welfare of all beings.".... Let me tell you about the Islam I know... An imam in Ladakh once told me that a true Muslim should love and respect all of Allah's creatures. And in my understanding, Islam enshrines compassion as a core spiritual principle, reflected in the very name of God, the "Compassionate and Merciful,"... Harmony among the major faiths has become an essential ingredient of peaceful coexistence in our world. From this perspective, mutual understanding among these traditions is not merely the business of religious believers — it matters for the welfare of humanity as a whole."

7 JOURNEY INTO SELF DISCOVERY™

The purpose of the *Journey into Self Discovery*™ (JiSD™) program is to integrate the insights and learning from my own personal journey with the tools referenced in the previous chapters. It would be neither reasonable nor useful to attempt to document or explain in detail how such integration would occur, but hopefully the following will provide a useful outline of what's involved.

David Whyte in this poem, *Traveller*, compared our whole being as "a travelling onward ghost that sees itself only in looking back, always just about to find a home, always a hairsbreadth from arrival, as if we were, after all, from the very beginning born far beyond ourselves." We can only see ourselves by 'looking back' and yet the best that we can do is always a hairsbreadth from arrival - in other words to be "who you truly are" cannot be achieved by a scientific, directive means. The best we can achieve would seem to be as close as the breadth of a human hair.

The JiSD program addresses how the three stages of The Holistic Self method coexist and participants leave with a Life-Path GPS blueprint that they and I collaboratively construct. The program objective is to help you discern:

- Where you are as a holistic person (body, mind and soul) today;
- How the 'Universal' energy and forces influenced your direction at the start of your life-journey and what appropriate adjustments need to be made to achieve your desired destination
- The tools and guidance system to employ that will enable you to plot your more compassionate and wise path forward.

Participating in JiSD is like being able to step off a roller coaster as it speeds along on a predetermined journey that you seem to have little control over. When we are faced by a crossroads on our life-path, it's usually wise to stop for a while to determine if we should continue as is, or switch to a new and more fulfilling path. As you progress through your journey into self-discovery, you will uncover aspects about yourself and elements of your approach to life that you will decide to retain; modify/repair; and discard/replace.

The adage: "If you always do what you've always done, you'll always get what you've always got." – aligns with Einstein's definition of insanity as, "doing the same thing over and over and expecting different results." Therefore, the JiSD program challenges participants to take inventory of how they are progressing with their life-plan and how the individual parts are harmonizing with each other to enable a happy, healthy and empowered future: "So if you want something different, you need to do something different".

In the last chapter I introduced the *Your Visible Personality (YVP)* and SQ21 tools to help you translate your behavior pattern (*Social Style*) into one of nine personality types (*Enneagram*). The central premise being; "if you can't measure it, you can't manage it." This book won't get into those subjects in any more detail because it was felt that you would likely be overwhelmed with information overload and end up more confused than when you started. Therefore, at this point I'd like to suggest if you would like a 'deeper dive' into any, or all, of the areas covered so far, it is recommended that you should go to *The Holistic Self* website and sign up for a free webinar or a coaching session.

One area that complements the JiSD program is the *Astrology natal report*. This was mentioned briefly in Chapter 5 and is a tool used in the JiSD program to help you discover the *nature* aspect of who you are. David Phillips, who wrote *The Complete Book of Numerology* said; "astrology is more than the mere studies of heavenly bodies. It is the ancient science of the study of the celestial bodies and their relationship to human life…Not only are these influences apparent in the formation of the weather and the tides, but also in farming and, most appropriately in human personality."

In cases where your date, time and place of birth are known, the JiSD program will utilize that data to create an astrology natal report specifically for you (not just a generic 'zodiac sign' printout). The process includes guided exercises that build on the natal report I provide to illustrate how the positions of celestial bodies (i.e. planets, etc.) at the time of your birth had a deep impact on both the known and unknown aspects of your personality. The natal chart along with the Social Style and Enneagram profiles (fromYVP) and your SQ21 profile (spiritual intelligence skills analysis) collectively work like the 4 satellite reference points for a GPS system. By explaining and illuminating how *nature, nurture and free-choice* combined to form a blueprint for your life up to the present day, you can better design your optimal path going forward.

The primary benefit is how the JiSD program helps you self-analyze what influences or decisions might have caused you to deviate from your original natal chart or soul-path and why. Sometimes people find that the path they are on is meeting expectations and the companions with them are proving to be very compatible, so they are content to continue on 'as is' from this point. In such cases some people simply want to verify what they feel instinctively about their life-path is correct, but are curious if there is some Universally forecasted 'bad weather' on their horizon. They say forewarned is forearmed and a little self-analysis may ultimately uncover some unforseen decay that if not treated may become toxic. Carl G Jung said, "Who looks outside, dreams. Who looks inside, awakens. "

JiSD is essentially a journey through one's multifaceted 'soul-labyrinth' to bring to awareness how your individual life-path blueprint was influenced at various stages, and how to architect your forward journey such that you perceive, act, and respond to life's events in the healthiest and most fulfilling way. JiSD has a number of key themes, and a major one is the integration of nature, nurture, and free choice. Another is the multiple attributes of your soul. As I mentioned earlier, the deepest longing of our soul is a yearning to be seen, and it gets our attention through extraordinary events in life such as moments of *awe* and deep sorrows. Those extraordinary events strengthen our spiritual muscle – which is so important when we are faced with our transformation process that will surely occur in the second half of life. Thomas Merton in his book *The Seven Storey Mountain* compared our souls to "athletes, that need opponents worthy of them, if they are to be tried and extended and pushed to the full use of their powers, and rewarded according to their capacity."

Inner happiness and peace contends with our *ego-self's* yearning to be someone other than our true self. We need to build the emotional and spiritual strength to resist artificial yearnings for toxic roles that societies, or other people, attempt to impose on us each day. When we re-discover our unique and authentic self that has always been present – but just well hidden from ourselves – others will want what we have and come to engage and learn from us. We can't force faith, love or knowledge. It is a 'pull' methodology. When we generate enough happy magnetic 'pull,' when our heart is singing, others are attracted to our happy-pulling force.

Are you afraid to face yourself? Does your inner voice ask this question; "If I expose my nakedness as a person to you – Do not make me feel shame?" It is unusual to find someone who has a clear view of him/herself, or who he/she really is underneath the social facade, or protective mask that we present to the world. Over time, we can often become more associated with the mask than the human being behind it, and even take on the attributes that society has etched onto our chosen style of mask. The majority of us take on some sort of protective exterior as an insurance policy against hurt, but that doesn't mean it's healthy.

There are parts of ourselves that we like to acknowledge and even promote as our best assets, but there are other areas within ourselves that we don't want to acknowledge or even try to hide for various reasons. However, there are other unknown-unknowns about ourselves that live in our Shadow – only glimpsed in moments of self-evaluation, but mostly pointed out to us by well meaning others. We all have 'blind-spots' - things about ourselves that we hold up as a virtue or positive attribute, which others can only see as self-deception.

Douglas Harding in his book, *On Having No Head* said, "I've lost my head but I've gained the world." We can't see our own face or head but we can see the world. We can't see ourselves but we can see others. However, the image of who we are in other's eyes is often distorted by the 'seer' lens. The challenge is to know which is the true 'mirror' that you should trust and which only offers a distorted reflection. To become an authentic and well-balanced individual, we need a way to view both our visible and invisible personality traits, and most importantly, to integrate them.

There are many situations where we can't show our true self and need to wear some type of armor to protect ourselves from a whole variety of social and relationship intrusions, manipulations, and personal harm. Our ego is our principal interior sentry that has assumed the charter to protect us ever since we were children. It is activated by instances that provoke a fear response – when we feel we were at risk emotionally, intellectually, physically and even spiritually. Some of the events today that automatically trigger our ego's alarm were only relevant during our childhood stage, but we have retained the response program, unchanged, through our teenage years and into adulthood.

A journey into self-discovery is about understanding your total or holistic self better, and without the self-deceptions that an unbridled ego-self promotes. In the JiSD program you will help you to:

- Uncover the complexities of your individual make up;
- Build more harmonious relationships,
- Gain more control over your life path;
- Achieve a reduction in life stress;
- Recognize your self-worth and spiritual purpose;
- And uncover hidden stores of energy.

To achieve greater self-fulfillment and relationship harmony, I found that I needed to uncover the answers to such questions as "Who am I?"; "Why do I behave the way I do?; "How can I love myself more?"; and also to discover why I was afraid to let people know my true self. To live a more fulfilled life – in body, soul, mind and heart, I discovered that I must learn to be happy living in my own skin. If you are conscious or suspect that you are living a conflicted life, it may be that like me your ego-self is governing your spiritual-self, instead of vice versa. This being the case, I propose you step off your roller coaster for a while and examine your life-path alignment relative to achieving your holistic self. In any event, I wish you every blessing and good fortune on your onward journey into self-discovery.

8 ANAM CARA – YOUR SPIRITUAL COMPANION

What is Anam Cara? It sounds poetic and many people have used the word casually as if it's a ticket to a 'spiritual realm'. Anam Cara is a Gaelic word that means "soul friend". Anam is "soul" and Cara is "friend". The Celtic tradition believes in a companion or spirit guide whom we can expose our vulnerability and reveal the inner self that we generally keep hidden.

It is also believed that our soul radiates around our physical body and sometimes is referred to as an aura. Our soul recognizes someone who is our Anam Cara when we meet them. "It could be a meeting on the street, or a party or a lecture, or just a simple, banal introduction, then suddenly there is a flash of recognition and the embers of kinship glow. There is an awakening between you, a sense of ancient knowing." John O'Donohue.

In everyone's life, there is a great need for a soul friend who always accepts you as you truly are and reflects your beauty and light back to you. In John O'Donahue's words, "...You are joined in an ancient and eternal union with humanity that cuts across all barriers of time, convention, philosophy and definition. When you are blessed with an

Anam Cara, the Irish believe, you have arrived at that most sacred place: home". I had found my 'home' when I was in Ireland.

Spiritual Direction is a form of Christian pastoral care and some of the most well-known and respected spiritual exercises were originated by St Ignatius Loyola. In 1521 Ignatius Loyola "was gravely wounded in a battle with the French. While recuperating, Ignatius Loyola experienced a conversion. Reading the lives of Jesus and the saints made Ignatius happy and aroused desires to do great things. Ignatius realized that these feelings were clues to God's direction for him. Over the years, Ignatius became expert in the art of spiritual direction. He collected his insights, prayers, and suggestions in his book the Spiritual Exercises, one of the most influential books on the spiritual life ever written. With a small group of friends, Ignatius Loyola founded the Society of Jesus, or the Jesuits. Ignatius conceived the Jesuits as 'contemplatives in action.[1]'"

The purpose of a spiritual direction is to help develop your discernment to be more attentive to God when you are actively participating in a Christian lifestyle. Some people dislike the term "spiritual direction" because it implies one person giving directions to another. Therefore, Spiritual Companionship is more widely used as it can be shared with or without any religion bias, which could be an obstacle for some people seeking to enter into a spiritual direction process.

This Christian concept of discernment to allow the Spirit to lead and guide our lives has evolved and is adopted by other faiths and non-faith alike. When John O'Donohue published the *Anam Cara: A Book of Celtic Wisdom* book, he created a more accepting concept of spiritual companionship,

[1] http://www.ignatianspirituality.com/ignatian-voices/st-ignatius-loyola/

which resonates widely with audiences who had previously been intolerant towards a particular religious language.

A Spiritual Companion or an Anam Cara is someone you can talk with confidentially about your emotional and spiritual life. Every aspect of your daily life affects your relationship with your holistic self, so day to day activities such as work, family, relationships, happiness, hurt and pain, joy, anger, etc. requires proper examination in a safe context. This is what you get during a spiritual companionship session. An Anam Cara in *The Holistic Self* program gently encourages you to examine events that led to self-doubt, confusion, fear, and anger, such that you are free to select your preferred entry point onto the path towards your Ulysses Paradox stage.

The Holistic Self – Anam Cara encounter involves:
- Staying with your questions and life struggles;
- Contemplation and reflection of you daily activities;
- 'Heart' cognition rather than 'Head' cognition - which includes reading and reflecting on sacred texts (of your choice and denomination, or none);
- Journaling insights that are illuminated during the heart cognition.

Meditation helps you understand how your mind works, and when you understand how your mind works you can begin to make purposeful changes to your life to improve it. Additionally, meditation improves your ability to objectively analyze your emotions, mental states, thought patterns, and responses to events that occur around you.

Contemplation on the other hand, is intended to allow your mind to rest in silence. Contemplation trains our mind towards a more complex thinking method – that is an ability to hold opposing concepts comfortably in balance. The complex thinking is also called non-dualistic consciousness; a pathway to compassion, or living *Beyond Religion* as the Dalai Lama actively encourages us to move toward.

Contemplation is a form of prayer or meditation in which a person seeks to pass beyond mental images and concepts to a direct experience of the divine – a spontaneous activity of the spirit. In meditation, one's imaginative and thinking power exerts some effort. Contemplation then follows to relieve one of all effort. Contemplation is the soul's inward vision and the heart's simple restfulness in God. The difference between these two conditions of the soul is like the difference between working and enjoyment of the fruit of our work; between receiving a gift and profiting by it; between the toil of travelling and the rest at our journey's end.

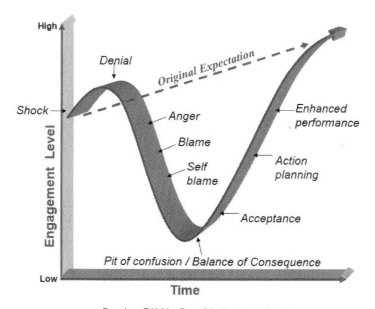

Based on: E Kubler-Ross, *"On Death and Dying"*

Trust is a foundation of a spiritual companionship. However, the phrase *'trust me'* has become something of a cliché these days and we forget that trust is something that is earned and not just something that is deserved or part of a package. Your Anam Cara will seek to build this trust and credibility by actions more so than words.

When you receive feedback from your Anam Cara you are in effect being asked to undergo a 'change process'. No one likes to have a mirror pushed in front of us (either by a loved one, a friend, or a boss at work) and our typical reaction is illustrated in the diagram.

Spiritual Companionship is not counseling. It is not therapy. It is not financial advice. It is for seekers who wish to enter a deeper, holistic relationship with their Self. Finding a spiritual companion is a mutual recognition. Both parties will have to feel connected to create a trusting, sacred place for intimate, non-judgmental sharing. Spiritual Companionship provides a safe, confidential space where you can explore a higher-self invitation into a deeper relationship.

The primary focus is recognizing that you are not alone and your Self is at the heart of daily life, sharing every experience with you. In *The Holistic Self* – Anam Cara context, you own the language and sacred texts of choice. The word 'companionship' indicates that your Anam Cara will encourage and accompany you through your Ulysses Paradox or on your spiritual journey. The Anam Cara does not direct you on how to solve your problems. Directing and problem solving are the goals of psychological therapy/counseling. Rather, your spiritual companion will listen attentively and alert your attention to activities or movements of your higher-self or the inner Spirit who is your ultimate "Spiritual Director."

Through attentive listening, observance of sacred silence, openness to inspiration, the slow process of discernment and deep gratitude, you will learn to rest in the Spirit and follow *Her* gentle guidance.

> "In the attitude of silence the soul finds the path in a clearer light, and what is elusive and deceptive resolves itself into crystal clearness."
> – Gandhi.

Your ego will object to you participating in the spiritual companionship because it feels that it will lose control and no longer be the center of attention and your life-path's 'project manager.' This is the reason why major religions teach 'die to self,' which I called the Ulysses Paradox, to allow the true 'center of attention' to be seen or heard. Only when you are emptied of your ego's fear can you discern your soul's life-path which will lead you towards living compassionately and in harmony with your environment and your authentic self.

Celtic Spirituality believes that "your soul knows the geography of your destiny. Your soul alone has the map of your future, therefore you can trust this indirect, oblique side of yourself. If you do, it will take you where you need to go, but more importantly it will teach you a kindness of rhythm in your journey." — John O'Donohue, *Anam Cara: A Book of Celtic Wisdom*. Gandhi gave similar advice.

9 DO YOU SEE ME?

Eckhart Tolle has been quoted on the divine purpose as saying that, "You are here to enable the divine purpose of the universe to unfold. That is how important you are!" For the longest time, I did not believe how important I was. Traditional Chinese culture taught me that I was insignificant. Being from an immigrant Chinese family in Thailand taught me that I was not the country's priority. Being a woman taught me that I was second-class to my male counter part. Trying to get a visitor visa to many countries in the world – especially in Europe – taught me that I was considered a low priority from an international citizen perspective. Therefore, it would be contradicting my well-developed rational and logic to accept as factual the words that Eckhart Tolle cited.

Yet, paradoxically, I do.

Christians may be familiar with Saint Paul's letter to the Corinthians (2Cor 12:9-10) "My grace is sufficient for thee: for my strength is made perfect in weakness. Most gladly therefore will I rather glory in my infirmities, that the power of Christ may rest upon me. Therefore I take pleasure in infirmities, in reproaches, in necessities, in persecutions, in distresses for Christ's sake: for when I am weak, then am I strong." I'm not quoting this passage to impose any Christian values on you. I'm quoting this passage to confirm Tolle's message above. I am 'important' (or strong) not because of my own 'boasting.' I know that I am important because the divine spirit, the eternal soul in me knows that I am important. My soul holds the secret to my destiny and she also knows that only me can fulfill that destiny.

In a few chapters of this book, I have shared with you the part of me that I normally would be afraid to share. I was afraid to show you who I really am because I'm afraid of what you might think of me. Upon reflecting I realize that this fear originates from my ego. That is understandable. It took my ego years of hard work to keep me from getting hurt. It is difficult for my ego to believe that it would not be hurt again. I'm not saying that I won't be hurt. I'm saying that the next time I'm hurt I know how to heal my ego.

My ego and I have developed an understanding. I told her that I love her and I need her to keep letting me know when I'm in danger and she should continue to suggest how I should get out of danger's way – but ensure that the danger is not relating to my former child-self persona that was once defenseless. I have learned to accept all aspects of me and better hold both my humanity and divinity in balance. I've learned that by myself I'm paradoxically not important and also most important because only I can fulfill my destiny. Both...and – I am weak because of my fear and yet I am strong because Grace makes me so.

I have shared my story in the hope that if you are like me, you may be hiding your gifted spiritual part, but you'll find courage to enter the Ulysses Paradox. If you so choose, you can perhaps trust me to accompany you on your journey to discover your beautiful, authentic and holistic self. According to Robert Cialdini, there is a rule for reciprocation:

"The rule says that we should try to repay, in
kind, what another person has provided us."
— Robert B. Cialdini, *Influence: The Psychology of Persuasion
(Collins Business Essentials)*

Many people have shown me kindness and compassion
during my own difficult yet enlightened journey into self-
discovery. I'd like to 'pay it forward' and be your Anam Cara
if that is the divine plan. Although my core faith is in
Buddhism, Hinduism, and Christianity, I believe that:

"Truth is one, though the wise call it by many
names". — Eknath Easwaran: *The Upanishads (Classic of
Indian Spirituality)*

The Dalai Lama has spent years traveling near and far to
promote compassionate living – or what he calls living
beyond religion. He taught us that we are human first and
foremost. We share our unity in humanity and in being One.
By sharing the same humanity 'trunk' at the core, we allow
each other to blossom into different fruits and flowers.

"Love and compassion are necessities, not
luxuries. Without them humanity cannot
survive." — The Dalai Lama, Beyond Religion .

The great rule of reciprocity states that if we take the
emotional risk to trust someone they will reciprocate in turn
and trust us. This is underpinned by a demonstration of
authentic love, kindness and an acceptance of each other for
who we truly are.

"The beginning of love is the will to let those
we love be perfectly themselves, the
resolution not to twist them to fit our own
image." — Thomas Merton, *The Way of Chuang Tzu*

Do you SEE me? Will you be my true mirror and reflect the beauty and light inside back to me? Will you let me be your true mirror too?

"Most people don't see things as they are. They see things as *they* are."
— Richard Rohr, *A Lever And A Place To Sand*

"Today, I set my heart right and allow myself to be re-formed into the person that I truly am. All by the Grace of God."
— Enda Eames

10 SUMMARY

"The non-permanent appearance of happiness and distress, and their disappearance in due course, are like the appearance and disappearance of winter and summer seasons. They arise from sense perception, and one must learn to tolerate them without being disturbed."
— *The Bhagavad Gita*

"The lovers cannot make the great moment of the oceanic oneness happened but together they can assume the inner stance that offers the least resistance to be over taken by the oceanic oneness that blesses their lives."
— James Finley, *Merton Palace of Nowhere*

Would going further with this be a good use of your time? To ensure you get a very good return from investing your valuable time in any self-growth or self-improvement program, it's often useful to determine up front if the program is likely to meet your needs or circumstances today. With that in mind, and before you proceed too far into making any further investment, I'd suggest you ask yourself if you are likely to fit into *The Holistic Self*™ vehicle to help you on your forward life-path?

The following are 10 key questions that I believe are useful to ask yourself to determine if you're ready to seriously explore your spiritual-self beyond what your ego demands. There are no right or wrong answers just ones to consider.

If you answer 'Yes' to at least 4 of the following questions, then you are likely to benefit from really putting some time aside to re-asses your life path and how the *The Holistic Self* program can assist you to navigate it better.

If you say 'Yes' to 6 or more of these questions, then you are at a key decision point in your life.

Therefore, if you can find a relaxed location – perhaps somewhere close to nature, where you can quieten your mind and shed some of your daily stress – ask yourself the following questions:

"Am I...?"
1. Seeking to understand myself better such that I can figure out why my life isn't running as smoothly as I'd like.
2. Feeling that there may be a higher meaning in my life than what I'm currently experiencing.
3. Remembering how I used to feel more alive within myself and positive about myself – but I seem to have lost a lot of that.
4. Confused about the way my relationships seem to deteriorate with some people unexpectedly, but also blossom unexpectedly with others.
5. Exploring the phenomena of why opposites seem to attract but then later on become agitated and even hostile towards each other.
6. Sad that my relationship is going through a constant struggle and I can't figure out why.
7. Convinced there is a higher meaning in life beyond accumulating things and status but don't have a way to allow both to coexist.
8. Disappointed that a lot of what we hear about Spirituality seems to be confined to some narrow philosophy, dogma or religious context.
9. Excited by the possibilities of how the human race can evolve towards a more sharing and caring philosophy and that I can be an example.
10. Curious about how our 'ego-self' and 'spiritual-self' can potentially co-exist and not seek to control our thoughts, actions, beliefs or life-path.

To continue onwards into the program, it is recommended you set aside some time on a specific day or days each week to start to record further reflections on the 10 questions above. This is a way for you to build a regular habit of claiming quality time to empower yourself and invest in your Journey into Self-Discovery.

As you take *your Journey*, be assured that you are among friends who have your best interest at heart and this will be confirmed through any future interaction with The Holistic Self's *"Journey into Self Discovery"* (JiSD) program, or through interacting with the The Holistic Self website at www.theholisticself.com.

ABOUT THE AUTHOR

Jamie Eames has always had a passion for helping people improve their lives. Her driving force has always been in the area of spirituality and how the human and spiritual elements of our lives coexist. She grew up in Thailand where she gained a science degree prior to moving to the USA where she gained a masters degree in information technology.

Jamie's gift is in helping others to self-heal through the combination of eastern and western spiritual insights, wisdom and her own unique methods. She has developed tools and resources that enable people who attend her programs to self-diagnose and self-heal the wounds received during their life-path.

Jamie has completed extensive studies in theology, spirituality, astrology, personality types, self-healing, and many other areas over the past two decade. She was employed by a number of leading ICT multinationals in technical, marketing and project delivery roles in the USA, Europe, Asia and Australia – where she now lives. She is currently focused exclusively on facilitating her new program *Journey into Self Discovery*.

This coaching and mentoring program has attracted significant attention from professional women and men who are seeking greater harmony, fulfilment and balance in their work, social and personal lives

BIBLIOGRAPHY

Ajahn Chah. (2011), Everything Arises, Everything Falls Away: Teachings on Impermanence and The End of Suffering. (Kindle Edition), Shambhala

Bourgeault, C. (2003), The Wisdom Way of Knowing: Reclaiming an Ancient Tradition to Awaken the Heart. John Wiley & Sons

Bourgeault, C. (2008), The Wisdom Jesus: Transforming Heart and Mind--A New Perspective on Christ and His Message. Shambhala

Bourgeault, C. (2010), The Meaning of Mary Magdalene: Discovering the Woman at the Heart of Christianity. Shambhala

Bruteau, B. (1971), Worthy is the World: The Hindu Philosophy of Sri Aurobindo. Associated University Press

De Mello, A., S.J. (1998), One Minute Wisdom. Gujarat Sahitya Prakash

Eames, E. (2013), Personalities at Work - How to quickly determine someone's Personality Type by simply observing their behavior. (Kindle Edition) 4R-CE

Easwara, E. (2007), The Upanishads. (Kindle Edition), Nilgiri Press

Estés, C.P. (2001), Women Who Run With The Wolves. (CD), Sounds True

Finley, J. (2003), Merton's Palace of Nowhere. Ave Maria Press; Revised edition

Finley, J. (2004), Thomas Merton's Path to the Palace of Nowhere. (CD) Sounds True

Finley, J. (2003), Christian Meditation: Entering the Mind of Christ. (CD) Sounds True

Frost, R. (2002), The Poetry of Robert Frost: The Collected Poems. Holt Paperbacks

Goleman, D. (2005), Emotional Intelligence: Why It Can Matter More Than IQ. Bantam Press

Grogan, B. (2000), Our Graces Life-Stories. Messenger Publications

Harding, D. (2012), On Having No Head. (Kindle Edition), The Shollond Trust

Hess, H. (2011), Siddhartha. (Audiobook), Trout Lake Media

Hess, H. (2012), Damian. (Kindle Edition), Dover Publications

His Holiness Dalai Lama, C., Cutler. (1998), The Art of Happiness: A Handbook For Living. Hodder & Stoughton

His Holiness Dalai Lama. (2008), In His Own Words: An Introduction to My Teachings and Philosophy. Hay House

His Holiness Dalai Lama. (2011), Beyond Religion: Ethics for a Whole World. (Audiobook), Random House

Helminski, K. (1992), Living Presence: A Sufi Way to

Mindfulness & the Essential Self. Penguin

Jacobs, A. (2003), The Bhagavad Gita. O Books

Johnston, W. (2000), Arise, My Love…Mysticism For a New Era. Orbis Books.

Kennedy, R. (2004), Zen Spirit, Christian Spirit: The Place of Zen in Christian Life. Continuum

Lama Surya Das, (1997), Awakening The Buddha Within: Tibetan Wisdom of the Western World. Bantam Press

Lewis, C.S. (2001), Mere Christianity. Harper Collins

Loehr, J. (2003), The Power of Full Engagement: Managing Energy, Not Time, is the Key to High Performance and Personal Renewal. (Kindle Edition), Free Press

Merton, T. (2010), The Way of Chuang Tzu. New Direction

Merton, T. (199), The Seven Storey Mountain. Mariner Books

Merton, T. (1979), Love and Living. (Kindle Edition), Farrar, Straus and Giroux

Michael, C.P. (2004), An Introduction to Spiritual Direction: A Psychological Approach for Directors and Directees. Paulist Press

Nouwen, T. (2007), The Way of the Heart. Darton, Longman & Todd

O'Donohue, J. (1996), Anam Ċara: Wisdom from the Celtic World. (CD) Sounds True

O'Donohue, J. (1999), Anam Cara: Spiritual Wisdom from

the Celtic World. Bantam Press

O'Donohue, J. (2000), Eternal Echoes: Exploring Our Hunger to Belong, Bantam Press

O'Donohue, J. (2008), To Bless the Space Between Us: A Book of Blessings, Double Day

O'Donohue, J. (2007), Benedictus: A Book of Blessings, Bantam Press

O'Murchu, D. (2002), Quantum Theology: Spiritual Implications of the New Physics. The Crossroad Publishing Company
Phillips, D. (1992), The Complete Book of Numerlogy. Hay House

Powell, J. (1969), Why am I Afrid to Tell You Who I am? Omnia Book

Pramhansa Yogananda. (1946), Autobiography of A Yogi. (Audiobook), Crystal Clarity Publishers

Raj, A.R. (1995), The Hindu Connection: Roots of the New Age. Concordia Scholarship

Rohr, R. (2004) The Enneagram: The Discernment of the Spirits. (CD), Center for Action and Contemplation

Rohr, R. (2013), Yes, And... Daily Meditations. Franciscan Media

Rohr, R. (2011), Breathing Under Water: Spirituality and the Twelve Steps. St. Anthony Messenger Press

Rohr, R. (2011), A Lever And A Place To Stand: The Contemplative Stance, The Active Prayer. St. Hidden Spring

Tacey, David. (2006), How To Read Jung. Granta Books

Ward, M. (2001), Beyond Chaos: The Underlying Theory Behind Life, The Universe, And Everything. Thomas Dunne Books

Whyte, D. (1994), The Heart Aroused: Poetry and the Preservation of The Soul in Corporate America. Double Day

Whyte, D. (2013), Pilgrim.(Kindle Edition), Many Rivers Press

Wigglesworth, C. (2012), SQ21: The Twenty-One Skills of Spiritual Intelligence. Selectbooks

DISCLOSURES AND DISCLAIMERS

This book compliments the Kindle equivalent version that is published in Adobe® Acrobat® Portable Document Format (PDF). "Adobe" and "Acrobat" are registered trademarks of Adobe Systems Incorporated in the United States and/or other countries.

All trademarks and service marks are the properties of their respective owners. All references to these properties are made solely for editorial purposes. Except for marks actually owned by the Author or the Publisher, no commercial claims are made to their use, and neither the Author nor the Publisher is affiliated with such marks in any way.

Unless otherwise expressly noted, none of the individuals or business entities mentioned herein has endorsed the contents of this eBook.

Limits of Liability & Disclaimers of Warranties

Because this book is a general educational information product, it is not a substitute for professional advice on the topics discussed in it.

The materials in this eBook are provided "as is" and without warranties of any kind either expressed or implied. The Author and the Publisher disclaim all warranties, express or implied, including, but not limited to, implied warranties of merchantability and fitness for a particular purpose. The Author and the Publisher do not warrant that defects will be corrected, or that any website or any server that makes this book available is free of viruses or other harmful components. The Author does not warrant or make any representations regarding the use or the results of the use of the materials in this book in terms of their correctness, accuracy, reliability, or otherwise. Applicable law may not allow the exclusion of implied warranties, so the above exclusion may not apply to you.

Under no circumstances, including, but not limited to, negligence, shall the Author or the Publisher be liable for any special or consequential damages that result from the use of, or the inability to use this book, even if the Author, the Publisher, or an authorized representative has been advised of the possibility of such damages. Applicable law may not allow the limitation or exclusion of liability or incidental or consequential damages, so the above limitation or exclusion may not apply to you. In no event shall the Author or Publisher total liability to you for all damages, losses, and causes of action (whether in contract, tort, including but not limited to, negligence or otherwise) exceed the amount paid by you, if any, for this book.

You agree to hold the Author and the Publisher of this book, principals, agents, affiliates, and employees harmless from any and all liability for all claims for damages due to injuries, including attorney, solicitor or barrister fees and costs, incurred by you or caused to third parties by you, arising out of the products, services, and activities discussed in this book, excepting only claims for gross negligence or intentional tort.

You agree that any and all claims for gross negligence or intentional tort shall be settled solely by confidential binding arbitration per The Institute of Arbitrators & Mediators Australia's commercial arbitration rules. All arbitration must occur in the municipality where the Author's principal place of business is located. Arbitration fees and costs shall be split equally, and you are solely responsible for your own lawyer fees.

Facts and information are believed to be accurate at the

time they were placed in this book. All data provided in this book is to be used for information purposes only. The information contained within is not intended to provide specific legal, financial, tax, physical or mental health advice, or any other advice whatsoever, for any individual or company and should not be relied upon in that regard. The services described are only offered in jurisdictions where they may be legally offered. Information provided is not all-inclusive, and is limited to information that is made available and such information should not be relied upon as all-inclusive or accurate.

For more information about this policy, please contact the Author at the e-mail address listed in the Copyright Notice at the front of this book.

IF YOU DO NOT AGREE WITH THESE TERMS AND EXPRESS CONDITIONS, DO NOT READ THIS BOOK. YOUR USE OF THIS BOOK, PRODUCTS, SERVICES, AND ANY PARTICIPATION IN ACTIVITIES MENTIONED IN THIS BOOK, MEAN THAT YOU ARE AGREEING TO BE LEGALLY BOUND BY THESE TERMS.

Affiliate Compensation & Material Connections Disclosure

This book may contain hyperlinks to websites and information created and maintained by other individuals and organizations. The Author and the Publisher do not control or guarantee the accuracy, completeness, relevance, or timeliness of any information or privacy policies posted on these linked websites.

You should assume that all references to products and services in this book are made because material connections exist between the Author or Publisher and the providers of the mentioned products and services ("Provider"). You should also assume that all hyperlinks within this book are affiliate links for (a) the Author, (b) the Publisher, or (c) someone else who is an affiliate for the mentioned products and services (individually and collectively, the "Affiliate").

The Affiliate recommends products and services in this book based in part on a good faith belief that the purchase of such products or services will help readers in general.

The Affiliate has this good faith belief because (a) the Affiliate has tried the product or service mentioned prior to recommending it or (b) the Affiliate has researched the reputation of the Provider and has made the decision to recommend the Provider's products or services based on the Provider's history of providing these or other products or services.

The representations made by the Affiliate about products and services reflect the Affiliate's honest opinion based upon the facts known to the Affiliate at the time this book was published.

Because there is a material connection between the Affiliate and Providers of products or services mentioned in this book, you should always assume that the Affiliate may be biased because of the Affiliate's relationship with a Provider and/or because the Affiliate has received or will receive something of value from a Provider.

Perform your own due diligence before purchasing a product or service mentioned in this book.

The type of compensation received by the Affiliate may vary. In some instances, the Affiliate may receive complimentary products (such as a review copy), services, or money from a Provider prior to mentioning the Provider's products or services in this book.

In addition, the Affiliate may receive a monetary commission or non-monetary compensation when you take action by clicking on a hyperlink in this book. This includes, but is not limited to, when you purchase a product or service from a Provider after clicking on an affiliate link in this book.

Purchase Price

Although the Publisher believes the price is fair for the value that you receive, you understand and agree that the purchase price for this book has been arbitrarily set by the Publisher. This price bears no relationship to objective standards.

Due Diligence

You are advised to do your own due diligence when it comes to making any decisions. Use caution and seek the advice of qualified professionals before acting upon the contents of this book or any other information. You shall not consider any examples, documents, or other content in this book or otherwise provided by the Author or Publisher to be the equivalent of professional advice.

The Author and the Publisher assume no responsibility for any losses or damages resulting from your use of any link, information, or opportunity contained in this book or within any other information disclosed by the Author or the Publisher in any form whatsoever.

YOU SHOULD ALWAYS CONDUCT YOUR OWN INVESTIGATION (PERFORM DUE DILIGENCE) BEFORE BUYING PRODUCTS OR SERVICES FROM ANYONE OFFLINE OR VIA THE INTERNET. THIS INCLUDES PRODUCTS AND SERVICES SOLD VIA HYPERLINKS EMBEDDED IN THIS BOOK.

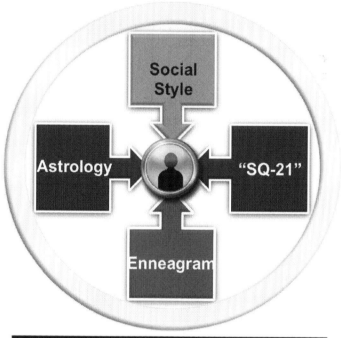

THE HOLISTIC SELF™

WWW.THEHOLISTICSELF.COM

Printed in Great Britain
by Amazon